THINGS THAT GO BUMP IN THE NIGHT

A COLLECTION OF TERRIFYING TALES!
Edited by Allison Dowse

Young**Writers**

A YOUNG WRITERS ANTHOLOGY

First published in Great Britain in 2005 by
Young Writers, Remus House,
Coltsfoot Drive, Peterborough, PE2 9JX
Telephone (01733) 890066
www.youngwriters.co.uk

Foreword

Young Writers was established in 1992 with the aim to promote creative writing in children, to make reading and writing more fun. This year we received many ghost stories from our young writers of today and within these chilling pages we have brought you a selection of the very best.

The entries we have selected highlight the children's keen interest and enthusiasm for the creation of the short story and are a showcase of the writing talents of the future. Together they will chill your imagination with their frightful and often funny tales of the supernatural.

Read on for an irresistibly hair-raising experience that will keep you creeping back for more.

Contents

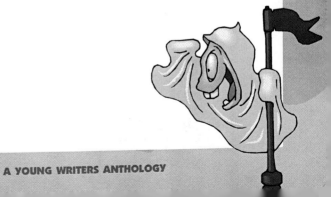

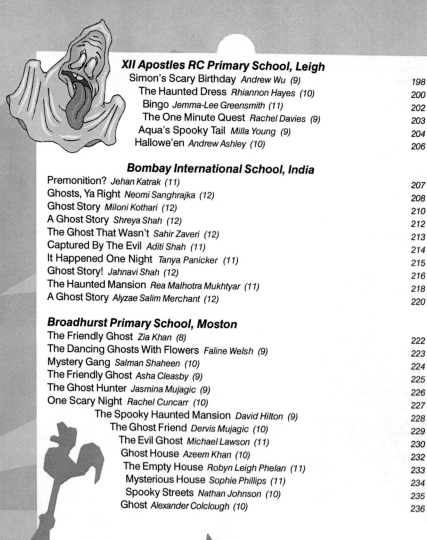

The Creative Writing

A YOUNG WRITERS ANTHOLOGY

Congratulations Belinda!
Your story wins you either a
fantastic family ticket to the
York, London, or **Edinburgh
Dungeons**.

Endless Nightmare

Imagine waking up to a world that's dead. No one alive but you. What would you do? Would you lie down and die with them?

I wake up from that nightmare not knowing I had awoken to the same destiny. The nightmare of my future. I call to see if anyone is up. No one answers, just like the dream. I search the rooms not knowing that what I am searching for is what I find.

Then I see them there, death in their eyes. I gasp in astonishment, it is exactly like it was in the dream. The rest couldn't be the same, surely everyone can't be dead?

I run outside to confirm my worst nightmare. To live it again. I knock on every door in the street, all open, all dead, just like the dream. This can't be happening. Is there anyone out there alive? I turn on the radio, nothing. I put on the TV, no one.

Have I woken up to a parallel universe where only I exist? Me and death. I run faster than before through the streets. Every street is isolated except for the bodies. All that lives there is death.

Imagine you wake up from a dream just to live it again. Imagine a nightmare where you can't wake up, the only escape is to die.

I know if someone is reading this there is life out there, but I also know if you're reading this, I am also dead.

Belinda Forde (14)

Diary Of Death

'My feet sank into the sand as I ran. Tears spilled out of my eyes, salty as the sea. On the horizon a whirl of pink, purple and orange marked the coming of morning. I hoped that I could hold on till then. The harsh wind blew against me, blowing my hair into a frenzy. The waves crashed, white foam licking at my feet and cold bullets of spume hitting my cheeks, sending cold spasms across my face. But suddenly agonising pain seared through my chest. I tried to scream, but nothing came out. I looked down and saw the tip of the knife, surrounded by fresh warm blood. Then there was darkness, never-ending black'.

I was choked up with horror at the diary entry. How could Elizabeth have written it? She was dead! She described in chilling detail her sad life and the strange things that happened in the house after she found the diary. My new house. This diary. And here was an account of her death. It was surreal. It was too strange, too frightening for the likes of me, Kelly, the frumpy but smart girl who wouldn't party, smoke or drink. With renewed fear I turned the page. I gasped. It was dated today! Shivers crawled up my spine as I read:

'Now I'm dead. I've got to haunt the next owners of the house. And then, when they're scared enough, they'll run. But I'll catch them. You see I have my little helpers, my little demons who can cross the threshold of this house into the outside world'.

Then the next words made me scream and run, run for my life:

'They're coming to get you Kelly. They're coming to get you and hurt you. They're coming to hurt you and kill you'.

You cannot run from death though. It will always catch up with you. Soon my blood splattered the sand and turned the sea foam red. You see that cursed diary claims the lives of all that read it. The only one who can write in it is the last soul that it took. Now you are reading my diary entry. So run, run, because the demons are going to get you!

Phoebe Lyons (13)

Well done Phoebe! You win a superb reading and writing goodie bag which includes a selection of books and a **Staedtler** Writing Set.

The Last Inn

It was a humid, unsettled night. Garry Eriksson sat in his room in the deserted Last Inn. He was investigating some odd reports. He worked for the UK Paranormal Investigation Team, based in Oxford University.

He checked his watch. Eleven thirty-four. In all the reports he had read, they all agreed that the activity began at twelve o'clock. He sighed and began setting up his Sony Digital Camcorder, checking the memory was blank and ready for the next three hours of filming and sat down. The reports also claimed that the disturbances had taken place in or around the wall to the right of the door. This was where most of his equipment was set up to observe. He heard the distant church bells tolling twelve and then it began …

All the lights in the room dimmed and then simultaneously exploded. The equipment began to register the readings vibrating wildly. Ethereal lights began dancing in the wall and Garry sat amazed as the display became more and more dazzling, suddenly stopping as a translucent hand reached out. One word was uttered, whispered, yet as loud as a car horn.

'Help!'

And then suddenly it was over and Garry came to his senses, leaping towards the camera and opening it, his hands shaking with excitement. An acrid smoke greeted his nostrils. It opened to show the memory sticks boiling, as if they had melted in horror of what its glassy eye had witnessed.

Liam Cooper (13)

Congratulations Liam! You win a superb reading and writing goodie bag which includes a selection of books and a **Staedtler Writing Set**. Well done!

The Deserted House

On her way home from school Fiona decided to take a short cut across a field where an old, deserted house stood. She opened the creaking front door and went in to look around. After climbing the old staircase, Fiona looked inside an old bedroom and suddenly her eyes were fixed on the image there in front of her. There were five white figures lined up to be executed and Fiona recognised each of these figures as members of her family, who had previously died.

Firstly she saw her grandfather place his head and his body onto the guillotine. The blade came down and chopped off his head and his body walked into thin air. The next three figures that received the same fate were her grandmother, her auntie and her uncle. The last figure had its back to Fiona so she couldn't recognise who it was.

All of a sudden the figure turned around and Fiona found herself staring at her own face! Fiona ran screaming out of the house and didn't stop until she reached home.

Sobbing, Fiona told her mum what she had just witnessed and asked her if she was going to die. Her mom sat Fiona down and said, 'There's been something I've been meaning to tell you since you were a young girl. When you were born you had a twin sister, but she unfortunately died when you were just three months old, so I believe the person you saw today was your sister Jodie.'

Zoe Nock (12)

The Skull

Hi, my name is David and I live with my mum. My dad works in Egypt, he's never here. This summer I'm going to my dad's. Earlier this year my dad sent me this voodoo doll skull. I'm taking it to Egypt with me.

I'm in Egypt right now! Look at this scorching sun. Dad! My dad!

I've now been here for ages and it's getting dark, my tent has no lights in it. All I want now is a light - a flash comes on from my bag. I open up my bag slowly and it's my skull voodoo thing. I hold it in my hand. It is floating. I'm dead scared. I follow it. I shouldn't do this but I follow it.

We come to a cave. I carry on following it and I am in a cave full of gold. I reach out to touch something. I feel something so I look round and there is a mummy. I run. My heart is beating so hard that it feels like it is going to fall out of my skin. More mummies keep coming from everywhere. I set out to sea on a tatty old boat.

I awake and am stuck on a beach. I'm back in America. I run to my house and finally I get in. I turn on the telly; the news. No one's on the screen. I scream, 'There's a mummy!'

Now I'm sat down. I'm the only survivor, I'm really scared …

Bethany Cooper (10)

The Tower

One stormy night Ash and David were running to shelter. After running and running they were exhausted and they came across a graveyard.

'Over there,' shouted Ash.

They both ran in the cemetery.

'Where should we go?' said David.

'In that tower,' replied Ash.

So David and Ash both ran towards the door but suddenly *smack,* they both hit the door head-on but it wouldn't open. Ash and David didn't give up, they carried on kicking the door when suddenly the door opened very slowly. Ash walked in not knowing what was going to happen.

'Well, are you coming in then?' said Ash.

'I'm not so sure about this place,' replied David.

'Stop your worrying,' shouted Ash.

So David was convinced it was fine, but that very moment the door slammed closed.

'I told you this place isn't right,' said David.

They both turned around, looking at the door. They both bumped into something so they slowly turned around …

'Argh!' shouted the boys. There was the Grim Reaper right in front of them. 'Please don't hurt us,' they shouted.

'Your time is up!' shouted the Reaper.

Ash and David ran for their lives. They got to the top floor and they looked around. It seemed like there was no Reaper in sight so they hid in the furthest and darkest corner. Suddenly they both fell through a trapdoor. 'Argh!' they shouted.

Then they were out of the tower and they ran home.

'I don't think that's the last of him,' said Ash.

Ashley Owen (10)

The Graveyard

Rebecca went to the graveyard to visit her nan's grave after school every day. But this time things turned out a little different than they had ever been before.

She was stood silently by the tombstone when suddenly she heard a strange, eerie noise. She looked all around her and saw a tombstone with no name or anything engraved on it. She thought nothing of it and carried on walking until she got home.

When she got home the door squeaked. She thought it was her dad, so she went up into her bedroom. There was something really scary, really frightening and the most dreadful thing she had ever seen. It was a *dead body!*

At first she thought it was a joke but it started to move towards her, faster and faster and faster. She ran and ran, there was nowhere else to go. She was trapped. She jumped over the dead body and shut the door. She went away and boy did she have at least two pages to write in her diary about this wondrous, dreadful day.

The next day she opened the door and the dead body wasn't there, she was scared at first, but she thought, *it can't kill me,* so she went to see her nan. She saw a tombstone right next to her nan's. It said 'Rebecca' on it and the dead body came up right behind her and ... *splat!*

And now no one dares go in the graveyard again because of 'Rebecca'.

Hannah Frost (11)

The Dead Come Back

One day Ollie and I were on the way to a party. We kept hearing noises but we didn't look round because we were too scared to look. When we got to the party it was still following us. We were glad to get inside because we were cold and scared.

When the party had ended we didn't want to go because the 'thing' might have still been still there and followed us and we were too scared to go out. We managed to get a lift home with our mum; our mum was cross because we didn't walk. We told her the whole story but she just got even more cross.

When we got home we went straight to bed because we were so tired and sleepy. We were so sleepy that we didn't remember about the 'thing'. That was good in a way because we got some sleep, if we'd remembered we would have been up forever!

In the morning me and Ollie walked to school, we were both talking about the 'thing' that we'd seen the night before. On the way to school we saw it again but this time we weren't scared. It was because we were in the sunlight and we stopped it coming nearer. We both grabbed it and, to our surprise, it was not a ghost, it was an old man.

But you never know, ghosts could be true, so keep a look out just in case you do see one …

Alex Ripley (10)

The Headless Ghost

On the 6th of May Timmy and Chaz are best friends. Timmy has blonde hair and blue eyes and loves wearing black clothes. Chaz has brown hair and green eyes and also loves black clothes.

On their way home from school they took a short cut through the field where they found a cave.

Chaz wanted to go in but Timmy didn't want to, but Chaz dragged him in. They found a door and opened it. They saw a ghost. It was wearing an old army uniform. It had a sword in its hand, but it had no head. It stepped out of the room and Chaz and Timmy ran home.

They went back to the field and looked around but they couldn't see him.

'There he is Chaz,' whispered Timmy.

'Come on run,' said Chaz.

'No!' shouted Timmy.

They snuck up to the ghost. It chased the two boys and got its sword out and hit one of the children, but the sword went through his arm.

When the children got home they found out the ghost couldn't hurt them so they went back and set a trap for it.

Chaz went to the cave and hid behind a rock. Timmy found the ghost and he ran back to the cave, the ghost followed him. Then they locked him back where he came from, so now the world is safe.

Daniel Sims (11)

Something Mysterious Behind The Bush

Hi there! My name's Christina Sanford. Last week was my 12th birthday. Yesterday my family and I moved to Scotland from Suffolk. Our new house is great and my new neighbour is so cute.

After we unpacked I played football with my brother Aaron for a while. Then Paul and his little brother David came out and they showed us around. Behind our houses were fields, but at the bottom of one there was a huge bush. Paul said it was great for exploring. David and him found something new every day.

The four of us did that. We explored, played games and it was so much fun. That night I was lying in bed and was distracted by a strange noise. I got up, poked my head out the door but there was no one there. I went back and got into bed.

5 minutes later I heard it again. This time I got up out of my bed and went to the window. It was coming from behind the bush at the back of the field.

It was freaky! I stared down past those fields for over 10 minutes. When it was quiet my bedroom door swung open with a bang. I turned round screaming. It was my brother. I could have killed him for scaring me. I think he was way more scared by the expression on his face. He was nearly crying.

'Chrissy, can I sleep in your room tonight?' he sobbed.

I was freaked out too so I replied, 'Alright then, but you have to go straight to sleep, OK?'

'Yes sir!' Aaron shouted.

We both laughed and got into bed and went to sleep with great difficulty.

The next morning we got Paul and David and discussed everything about last night. It was simple because they'd heard it too. We decided to skip adventures for one day.

A week later the noises came back and we had had enough. We went down and looked. We were shaking. There were skeletons dancing around a body. They captured sight of us in the corner of their eyes and chased us the whole way home. It was frightening, as if we were running for dear life.

We then looked out the window in the morning and there was no sign of anything from last night. I had had enough. I was going to find out what was going on at night. David and Aaron kept watch and Paul and I slowly went through the bush and watched the skeletons. Then Paul fell off the bush and we ran past them but they didn't care this time and all we heard was, 'Cut! What are you kids doing here again? You've ruined the 3rd take,' said a tall, weird man.

We asked what was going on. And it wasn't a sacrifice ritual at all, they were trying to make a film. Paul and I laughed about it the whole way home and when David and Aaron woke up we told them and they laughed so hard they were crying. But they were also glad it wasn't some ancient legend.

3 months later the film came out so Paul and I took our brothers to see it, and I'll admit it was good. But so much had happened in the space of a few days of just moving in, but honestly, I couldn't have found better friends.

Laura Wilson (14)

Ghost!

Not long ago there was a boy called Dan. He was 11 and his grandad had recently passed away. Dan had short dark brown hair, his hobbies were skateboarding and footie. He also had two younger sisters called Sarah and Jess. He got on really well with Jess, but struggled with Sarah.

One evening Dan had a nightmare about wandering around in a graveyard, and suddenly he stopped and heard the sound of gunfire, so he started to run as fast as he could. Then, as he got further, he saw a dead body on the pavement. He carried on running but heard his name being chanted in a ghostly-sounding sort of voice.

The next morning he decided to go back to the graveyard to find out what happened in his nightmare. Further on in the graveyard he reached a gravestone. Whose gravestone was it? It looked new and he could hear voices coming from inside it. He got really scared so started to run as fast as he could. He ran and ran, but then he woke up …

He went out of his room and downstairs into the kitchen to get a drink and then felt something on his shoulder. He turned round and saw a ghost. It was the ghost of the man that was lying dead on the pavement as he was running out of the graveyard …

Hannah Harbour (10)

Orb Retirement

Amy glanced at her watch - 10.43pm. She wandered upstairs to her bedroom. Opening the door Amy yawned a long yawn. She stared drearily at the darkened room. Something white shot across it. Amy gasped. She switched on the light and the room suddenly turned friendly.

Amy lay awake while visions of white circles jetted across her mind like they had across the room. She switched off the lamp and the room grew eerie. Something tapped her face. She opened her mouth to scream but closed it again. The white orb hovered in front of her. It grew.

A young girl of Amy's age stood at the end of the bed.

'Hi,' she greeted.

Amy couldn't speak.

'Hello,' giggled the girl. 'My name's Cally and you are?'

'Oh my goodness!' breathed Amy.

'Er … hello Miss, oh my goodness!' giggled Cally.

'Um … name's Amy,' replied Amy.

'I'm a ghost, in case you didn't notice,' Cally blurted.

'Cool!' exclaimed Amy.

Cally stated, 'I suffocated in this bed.' Cally pointed to Amy's bed. 'I want to go to the upper dimension but I'm stuck, can you help me?' asked Cally.

'Um … all right,' smiled Amy.

'Great! All right, I want you to open this window,' announced Cally, as she pointed to the window.

Amy did so and cold air cut in like a knife against Amy's cheek.

'Thank you ever so much!' exclaimed Cally as she faded. 'Goodbye!' Cally disappeared.

Amy slammed the window shut. A white orb flew across. *Oh no, not again!* thought Amy.

Sara Nicholas (10)

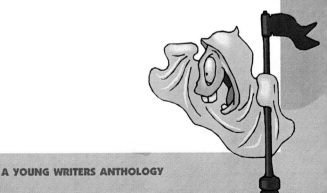

Amber Eyes

'Was that you Mum?' No one replied. She sat up and looked around. She could only see a pair of amber eyes. 'Stop that Bran, it's really not funny.'

Dixie got out of bed and went downstairs to join the others.

'Mum! Mum! I saw another pair of amber eyes.'

'So did I, they're everywhere. Mum, what are we going to do?' said Bran.

'I've got an idea. Where do you mostly see these amber eyes then?'

'In Dixie's room,' called Bran. So they all went upstairs into Dixie's room.

Suddenly, the door slammed shut and then locked them in.

'Look! It's a little girl with amber eyes,' shouted Dixie.

The girl then lifted up a dagger and screamed out loud, 'Why should I be drowned because my mother and father did not like me, or love me?'

Dixie had a thought in her head. 'Stop!' she yelled. 'All you need is to be loved and have a family. Why don't you be in our family?'

The girl suddenly dropped the knife and came back to life. 'Thank you, you have broken the curse which was upon me,' she said in a soft voice. 'I shall live with you and by the way, my name is Tegan.' She walked towards them and gave them a hug and a kiss.

'My name's Dixie, he's Bran and that's our mum.'

'Yes I know all of your names,' said Tegan calmly, 'and I know that you're all of my family.'

Shannon Cliff (10)

A Cup Of Sugar

'Bye Mum, have a nice time,' said Naomi.

'Come on inside,' said Grandma May.

Naomi walked up to the spare room and unpacked her suitcase.

Naomi's mum had gone on holiday and she missed her very much. To spend time with her horrible grandma and her uncle would be dreadful.

'Hello!'

Naomi turned around suddenly. 'Who's there? Uncle Bill, are you playing tricks on me again?' She just sighed and got on with it.

After she'd unpacked her bag she went downstairs to see what was for dinner. Her gran and uncle had left a note on the dining table to say that they'd gone to the supermarket. She was browsing through the cupboards. *That's odd, the sugar was just there,* she thought to herself. *Something is fishy about this house.* She was about to walk out the kitchen when she saw two shadows standing by the tin of sugar.

'Please!' she heard someone say. She ran upstairs and hid under the bed and waited for her grandma and Uncle Bill to come back. She told her grandma what had happened.

'Nonsense,' her grandma said. Her gran didn't believe in ghosts.

After dinner Granny May went to bed and Uncle Bill talked to Naomi in quiet.

'I believe this house is haunted. I heard recently that one couple went round to a new neighbour for a cup of sugar. The man took them in and murdered them, but this man used to live in this house where the couple were murdered,' said her uncle.

'Oh my God, how tragic, but I've got a plan,' said Naomi. 'They want the cup of sugar don't they, so give it to them!'

Naomi Qureshi (11)

The Forbidden House!

It was a dark, gloomy night. The wind was howling at the Teatrees' house. Alice was looking out of her bedroom window one night, tapping the windowpane, when suddenly she saw a shadow outside her bedroom door. It came closer and closer and closer when she saw a bat swoop past her window. She turned around and the shadow was gone.

Alice couldn't sleep that night. She tossed and turned but it was no use. She kept on thinking about that shadow. Who was it? What was it? And where was it now?

'Argh!' There was a scream. Alice went into her mum and dad's room and found that her mum, Heather, was gone. There was blood everywhere and the bedroom window was open. The kidnapper had taken Heather to a forbidden house. The house sat crookedly high in the old oak tree - dirty, gloomy and frighteningly dark.

'Help! Help!' cried Heather. 'Anyone please help.'

But there was no sign of anyone. The kidnapper went up the ladder and hung Heather over the edge and threatened to kill her if she didn't tell him where her famous diamond was. Heather wouldn't as it was worth £10,000,000 and used to belong to her dear old grandmother. So he hung her over the edge even further and all of a sudden he dropped her. Heather was gone, gone to a better place.

The kidnapper quietly went away He's left this town now but beware, he could be heading for yours!

Lucy Threader (10)

Spooked

Whip! went the wind against Hannah and Mccoy's faces as they opened the rusty iron door.

'One, two, three, argh!' they wildly shouted, as they charged into the terrifying house.

Inside it was like a sewer and didn't smell much different. There were cobwebs everywhere and books strewn on the floor and I won't even tell you about the windows, though once they were probably the prettiest in the town.

As Hannah turned round her long blonde hair hit Mccoy's right arm and they both screamed, not from the hair but there was a big black cart coming their way and before they could move it picked them up.

'You don't think this house is really haunted do you?' asked Mccoy who was usually the brave one.

'Ssshhh! I can hear something, can you?' asked Hannah.

'Well I certainly can,' went a strange laughing voice. *'Ha! Ha! Ha! Ha!'*

'Was that you?' asked Hannah. *'Mccoy! Mccoy! Argh!'*

A dark silhouette had formed in front of her.

'Are you gonna get off this ride now?' It was only the haunted house owner.

'What took you so long? Anyway, it's our turn to dare Otty and Rosie now,' said Mccoy. They both looked at each other.

The haunted house!

Ottilie Baker (10)

The Gloomy House

It was a dark, stormy night as Bill walked down an old, empty road on his own. The wind was howling, it was lightning and, most of all, he felt as though he was being followed.

'Argh!'

He turned his head towards the house the scream came from. It had a long driveway up to an old castle-like mansion with bats and owls on the rooftop.

Bill knocked on the double doors which were dark, and they opened with no one to welcome him.

He went up the steps that had a brown banister full of cobwebs. He carried on and heard some tapping.

'Eee, eee.' It was *rats.* Bill hated rats but he wanted to carry on and be a hero.

He got to the top floor, and was going to work down the house and find the person that screamed. He stepped on a rug, it lowered, he was falling down a slide through to the cellar. He came out onto a metal board and got locked on it.

He looked up and saw a man with a black cloak holding a knife.

'Argh!' He was stabbed and an outsider heard and went to investigate …

George Pitts (10)

The Noise

A full moon glared down on one house in the cul-de-sac that night. The clock had struck midnight and one boy lay awake on Pheasant Cross. He couldn't get to sleep because of shadows and tapping all through the house.

He had called for his mum many times but she had not responded at all, so he lay there under his quilt because he felt so much safer there. The shadows on his bedroom wall were moving about and the noise was getting louder.

He lay still for a few moments in bed, then he peeped out of the curtains and a street lamp flickered for a few seconds and then went out. The boy went back to sleep and didn't hear the noise for a long time. After an hour or so there was tapping again.

He looked and there appeared to be nothing so it was left as a mystery.

Ben Moylan (10)

The Bad Journey

On an old road in the middle of nowhere five friends were driving in a camper van. They were lost. It was getting extremely misty, plus it was getting darker and darker and darker. They drove slowly on the sea front. The waves were crashing on them every so often. They searched for somewhere to stay. It was getting spooky.

Suddenly, with hard searching, they saw a church in the distance, in a lonely field with graves scattered in front of it. They saw trees in the surroundings and decided to camp there for the night. They started making their way into the field. They set up a campfire and huddled around it. It started to get creepy.

Suddenly the trees fell dead and heads started popping out of graves. The full moon appeared, wolves started to howl and the clock struck midnight. There was a great scream. The campfire went out and a dead vicar came out of the church. The five friends fainted.

They woke up in the van. They looked who was driving. It was the dead vicar …

Jake Grayshon (10)

Lisa's Terrifying Night

As she crept through the house in her dressing gown and slippers, holding a candle for light, following the long corridor to find the toilet, she heard a creak, she stopped ... then she heard footsteps. The sound was quite blurred in the distance but as she wandered past the corridor the sound got louder and clearer, almost as if it was following her.

Lisa was getting quite scared and then she suddenly felt a cold hand on her shoulder. She looked at her shoulder and there was nothing there, but she could still feel the hand. Lisa turned around and screamed as she saw the door at the top of the stairs opening and her mother peered at Lisa.

'What's all the fuss over Lisa?' she asked. 'It's only me!' she announced.

'I ... I ... It's nothing really,' Lisa said timidly.

'And what on earth are you wandering the corridors for at this time of night anyway?' her mum asked.

'I just wanted the loo,' Lisa said.

'Well, it's all the way back there darling, come on, I'll take you,' her mum said.

They got to the toilet and to their rooms perfectly fine, but Lisa didn't sleep that night and had to rush to her mum's room to sleep there.

The next night Lisa woke her mum to ask her to take her to the toilet. As they were making their way across the corridor they heard the creaks and footsteps and both felt a cold hand on their shoulders ...

Catherine Williams (11)

Death Day

In the moonlight a werewolf appeared from the middle of nowhere. Millie ran and ran until she couldn't run anymore and she collapsed onto the floor in the middle of the park. She felt a wet nose, dripping with blood from its last victim, nuzzling at her. Suddenly she felt a searing pain running down the side of her as she thought that it was going to leave her alone, but it didn't, it ate her alive …

Later that night the werewolf struck again by Dead Man's Lake, the lake that has ghosts and souls in it. This time it struck another teenager called Billy. He pushed him deep into Dead Man's Lake. He felt an icy cold hand grab his leg; Billy looked down, terrified that he would run out of air. He saw white mist in the water creeping up to him and came face to face with it. Slowly it started smothering him. Suddenly he felt an icy cold hand grab his throat. He choked and struggled. No one ever saw him again.

Dawn was breaking and the werewolf was heading back to its den. When he finally got there he saw that his den had been destroyed and couldn't get it back in. Then the sun shone right on him. He started trying to get shelter but everywhere he went he always got that sunshine. He started to shrivel like bacon and turned into ashes. The ground opened and Hell was revealed.

Emma Birch (11)

The Clown

A couple had a baby girl and they painted the baby's room pink. The next day while they were out they saw this really nice clown to hang over the cot in the baby's room, so they bought it. But that night the mum heard feet running in the baby's room and when she went in all the furniture was moved. She looked at the clown and all she could see was a great big grin on its face.

The next night the dad heard feet running up and down in the baby's room and when he went in all the furniture was moved again. All the dad could see was this great big grin from the clown.

The next night they heard the baby choking so both the parents ran into the baby's room and the baby had a button in its mouth and it was from the clown's costume, so then the parents knew it was the clown. They burnt every last bit of him, but a button was left under the cot.

Two years later the parents were decorating the baby's room again. They went out looking for stuff and they found some nice pictures to hang on the wall. They hung them up, but the clown hadn't died so every night the clown was in a different picture, waving at them with a huge grin on his face.

Billie Wibberley (11)

The Funny Ghost

Once upon a time a family lived together in a town called Wattsfield. There was a boy, Jamie, who moved in with his grandparents.

One day Jamie saw a man hammering up posters in the park. It was all about a fair. Jamie took one look at the poster and wanted to go. He made a quick dash for his grandparent's house and they said yes.

When the fair arrived he quickly went on the ghost ride. A ghost popped up but nobody screamed, they all laughed because it looked as if it was pulling silly faces. When they got out the ghost came and asked Jamie if he would be its friend because he was the only person who didn't laugh at him.

One of the passengers told the manager it wasn't very good because there was a ghost who wasn't scary. They brought out a scary thermometer and made the ghost scream. The thermometer showed 'very funny' so it was sent away.

The ghost asked if it could stay with Jamie.

'Of course,' answered Jamie.

The ghost drifted round with Jamie. When they came to the mirrors Jamie made the ghost cover its eyes and then uncover. As the ghost did so he saw himself in the mirror. He thought it was another ghost coming to attack him and fled out of the hall screaming. The manager saw him and re-employed him, thinking it was another ghost. For his help, the ghost remained firm friends with Jamie forever.

Toby Melville (7)

Alone!

It was the first time he'd stayed home alone late at night and he was a little freaked out. He kept hearing noises around the house and thought he could see shadows creeping on the walls. He knew his mind was playing tricks on him, so he turned the TV on to try and take his mind off being alone.

Suddenly there was a loud tapping on the window that made the boy jump. He ignored it at first but then it happened again. The boy turned the TV up but then a ghostly, echoey voice came from outside.

'Look out the window!' it said.

The boy huddled into the couch, trying not to make a noise in hope that the thing outside would go away.

'Look out the window!' came the spooky voice again.

In the end the boy slowly and cautiously got up from the couch and ran to the phone, but when he picked it up, the line was dead. Suddenly the lights started to flicker. A chill entered the room and the boy froze in fear of what was behind the window.

'Look out the window!' shouted the voice once again, but the boy screamed and ran up to his room and locked the door.

Suddenly there was a tap on the window and when the boy looked up he saw two red glowing eyes that stared right into his. The boy screamed and fell to the floor and he never saw the light of day again.

Amy Cutler (14)

Spooktacular

'Hey, you guys,' said Timothy.

'What?' Timothy's brother John replied.

'The new ride House Spooktacular is open for a free try out!' said Timothy, better known as Tim.

'Let's go! said Andy.

'Can't,' said John, 'sorry.'

'Why?' asked Andy.

'Homework.'

'We'll go tomorrow,' said Tim.

The following day they queued up to go in. They collected their laser tasers laser guns.

'Whoa,' Tim said as they went in.

The walls had cobwebs all over them, slime oozed down the walls.

'You'll never escape House Spooktacular!' a spooky voice cried, the sound bounced off the walls.

A bit scared, they walked on in silence.

Ten minutes later a ghost appeared in front of them. 'Leave now,' cried the ghost.

'Why?' they asked.

'For I am the spectre of the ride!'

Zwoop!

'It's real!' screamed Tim. 'Run!'

But before they had a chance to run, all but Tim fell through a trapdoor.

'Let them out!' bellowed Tim.

'You'll have to destroy me then,' screamed the spectre.

Zwoop!

'That the best you can do?' said the spectre.

Zwoop!

'Argh!' screamed the spectre.

The ghost vanished.

'John?' called Tim. 'Andy?'

'Over here,' he heard Andy call.

Outside they handed the guns back.

'Well, I'm just glad that's over with,' Tim said.

'So am I,' Andy and John chorused.

'That's what you think!' a spooky voice whispered …

Warren Strong (11)

Someone's In My Bedroom

One night when Ann went to bed she heard strange noises coming from downstairs but she didn't know what they were. Ann had never been scared at night until now.

The next night, before she went to bed, she stroked Benji her dog. Benji followed her upstairs. When they got in Ann's bedroom the dog *froze,* stared at the foot of the bed then raced downstairs with a whimpering sound as if he'd seen something. Ann was horrified so she raced downstairs too, crying for her mother. Ann's mum, Ann and Benji went up in the room. Ann's mum tucked her in and gave her a goodnight kiss, then she left the room with the dog.

In the middle of the night Ann awoke hearing her bedroom door creak open.

'Mum, Dad? Dad is that you?' she whispered.

After waiting for a while she fell asleep.

When she woke up again she could see a man at the foot of her bed. As her eyes adjusted to the dark she could see a man *staring* at her. Ann's heart skipped a beat. This thing was not her dad, for it was a ghost … It came towards her slowly, still gazing at her with those evil eyes and … *chop!* Ann's head rolled off her pillow and thumped onto the floor …

Nicola Lewis (12)

The Hand

When Mariah was asked if she wanted to go on the school trip to Scotland she wasn't sure. Mariah was a timid person who was full of dark, disturbing secrets of the past. Eventually she was persuaded by her friends to go. Little did she know it was the part of Scotland where the dark secrets began . . .

Looking out the coach window she remembered the last trip to Scotland which turned her life upside down. Then to her horror she saw . . . the lake.

The next day Mariah sneaked down to the lake. For some strange reason she had an urge to row out in a boat to the middle of the lake. Sitting looking at the rippling water she remembered what had happened on that tragic day.

She was only eight when it happened. What could she have done to help? Her parents had been happily rowing, then suddenly dragged mysteriously into the water. All she had seen was a white ghostly hand fly out of the water and grab them. She'd sat in that boat for three hours just waiting for her mum and dad to pop back up, smiling. But it never happened. She wished with all her heart it would, but deep down she knew her parents were dead.

Suddenly out of nowhere a lacerated hand, identical to that which had killed her parents, shot out of the water and dragged her under. She had followed her parents' horrific fate.

And she was happy.

Charlotte Abbott (11)

The Secret Of Demon's Bay

From the moment I stepped up on the old castle's doorstep and rang the rusty bell I knew I was doomed. The ancient building towered above me, a huge shadow of black against the dark velvety sky. The stars glimmered against the vast darkness, like a black tablecloth with silver glitter, shimmering at every touch of light, the moon, a giant glowing ball.

Spray hit me like hail, hard and sharp. A single nightingale on a branch, voice as smooth as silk, as sweet as syrup. A mournful song filled with sadness and sorrow as if there's no hope for tomorrow, as if no one but me is alive on Earth. A sudden creak interrupted my dreams. The door was opening …

Larischa de Wet (10)

Arghh! Zombies

On a dare I went to the graveyard to the old oak tree by Mr James' grave. I heard the clock on the church strike midnight.

I felt a chill go down my spine. It started to thunder and lightning that was followed by a downpour. I looked up at the sky as I thought it couldn't get worse. I saw a full moon that really freaked me out and I looked back down and I saw the most terrifying sight I'd ever seen.

Thick green hands were popping out of the graves and they had no fingers. I turned and said to myself, 'It's not real.' I felt something hit me on my shoulder, I looked, it was an acorn. I felt another tap, I looked up, it was a zombie.

I ran and ran and then I tripped and a man came and shot all the zombies - I was saved! I never went to the graveyard again.

Max Walker (11)

The Well

I was walking out to the car and when I started driving down the road I saw a girl in a graveyard.

'Little girl, what's your name?' I said shocked.

'Katy Rose, but please could you take me home?'

'Yes of course, but where do you live?'

'The old farm on Demon Street.'

'OK.'

When I took the girl home the farm was misty and lonely. She went inside and appeared at the top window and suddenly a bag went flying over her head. I ran upstairs to help her, but there was nobody there.

Later, I drove past the graveyard and there was a man putting something down the old well. It took me a couple of minutes to realise that it was the little girl. I panicked, but it was too late. He had closed the well.

I drove back home and told my friend about the girl. She asked me her name.

'Katy Rose,' I told her.

'I remember reading about an article of a Katy Rose. Her parents murdered her.'

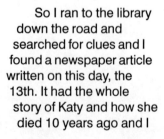

So I ran to the library down the road and searched for clues and I found a newspaper article written on this day, the 13th. It had the whole story of Katy and how she died 10 years ago and I saw a picture of the girl, the same girl I had seen, but she looked evil.

Every time the bells at the graveyard rang it sounded like she was screaming.

Callum Tolson (11)

Trick Or Treat

In the year 2004, the day before Hallowe'en a group of friends were planning a route for where they would go to trick or treat for the next day. They all met in the spooky forest. There they showed each other their brand new costumes, some were witches and werewolves and others were goblins and ghouls. But there was one person at the meeting that they didn't know. Everybody else was at the meeting who should have been there, the creature had a white rugby mask, a red and black cloak, also skeleton hands that weren't gloves.

One of the oldest members said, 'What is your name and what are your doing here?'

The creature replied, 'I am the ghost of Hallowe'en.'

Frankie, the oldest said, 'Ha, ha, very funny, what you going to do, rugby tackle us or something?'

But that was a big mistake. Hallowe'en then pulled out a dagger the length of your hand to your elbow and he whispered, 'Do not taunt me or you shall never see daylight again.'

Jack said, 'Frankie, be quiet now. I think it's being serious.'

Everybody froze with fear as Hallowe'en moved closer to a tall member with a scream mask on. He put the dagger into Hubert's hand, suddenly Hallowe'en jumped on Hubert and started strangling him …

Everybody started running and then Hallowe'en shouted,
'All of you shall pay the price for entering spooky forest!'

    The next day, Hallowe'en, the group decided to stick to
the route and not to go wandering off. But the group did
not remember that Hubert had had a copy of the route!
That meant that Hallowe'en knew where they were going.

    That night they met in the middle of Creaky Street.
They slowly moved around the houses, every house they
went to the group had a different watchman looking out for
the terrifying Hallowe'en. At the end of the night they met
back up on Creaky Street counting their sweets. They
forgot to ask anybody to watch out! So quickly and
quietly Hallowe'en snuck up on one member at a time until
there was one left, Jack. Instead of taking Jack away,
Hallowe'en bit him, injecting Hallowe'en poison into him.
The only way to survive was to give his soul up to the Devil
and become the next Hallowe'en . . .

Samuel Knott (13)

Sacrifice

She was there again. Her steely eyes penetrated me with cold precision. As eager to rip and tear as always. Hungry; I could see her fangs glint in the corner where she crouched. I beckoned to the small child behind me.

Shivering, the tiny infant tottered into the room. Like me, he could sense her presence. Eyes bright with fear, his hands shook as he clutched his precious teddy to him.

As the child came to stand beside me, her attention slid slowly from me to the toddler. Her silver eyes, without pupil or iris, appraised this new meal.

I nudged my brother forwards. He tiptoed towards her corner. Whimpering, he laid Tim at her feet then scuttled back and together we disappeared through the trapdoor, back to the sanctuary of the house.

From the safety of the broom cupboard we listened to the noises drifting down from the cave-like attic. A scraping, rasping sound as she dragged her spiny tail across the floor towards her prey. We pictured brave Tim, motionless, frozen with terror. Then we heard a ripping noise as though someone had torn a piece of cloth apart. Tim was dead, another victim of the Volem. His remains (a few threads and two button eyes) joined the pile of fluff that the Volem had accumulated. Her hunger was satiated. I offered a prayer to her, asking her to stay in her attic and spare us for one more day. We were running out of teddies.

Kaitlin Lloyd (14)

Death By Conscience

She walked down the eerie lane, the pathway leading to unknown dangers and troubles haunted by a guilty conscience and stressed mind.

The lights flickered and went out. The girl barely noticed them as she followed an arrow, As Macbeth followed the dagger to kill King Duncan. Around and around, up and down, the arrow went till it stopped at a door and vanished. The girl hesitated and the room beyond the door called to her like the hounds of Hell calling to an evildoer. She pushed open the door and saw Emily lying there in a pool of blood and the scene changed to that of a car, with Emily's body inside, mangled and deformed and beside her, a place where the driver should have been.

Emily sat up and the girl screamed. Emily was dead, yet she got up, mangled and deformed as she was, covered in blood and walked over to the girl. She took the girl harshly by the wrist and dragged her to the car. The girl struggled, pulled away, but the deceased Emily was too strong and pushed her down in the driver's seat. 'I'm not the only one dying today,' she screeched and laughed maniacally.

The girl shuddered and couldn't breathe - her lungs felt like they were being crushed and she gasped and gulped and finally, lay still.

In the hospital the doctor looked up from the girl's mangled body and said, 'I'm sorry, we've lost her.'

Laura Summerfield (14)

The Ghosts Of The Middle Ages

I ran and I ran, panting deeply, my heart pounding against my chest. I couldn't stop running, even for one split second, not in a situation like this anyway. They were after me, big and dangerous were the Ghosts of the Middle Ages.

My friends had told me to stay away from them but I didn't believe them, I never do really. And there I was running away from these terrible spirits.

I had reached the gates, at last, after running from one end of the wood to the other was most tiring. I opened them with great ease and relief.

Once I was out I could rest. I sat down and enjoyed the moment of relaxation. But not for long anyway. It was ten to nine already and Dad would be worried about me.

I stood up and walked all the way home in the dark. When I got there, we had a blazing row and then he slapped me on the cheek. It started to bleed heavily. I explained to him where I'd been but he called it a load of lies and sent me to my room.

I didn't go to my room, I picked up the camera and went back to the wood. I would show him that the ghosts were real and alive, well partly.

When I got through the gates the ghosts reappeared. Then I shot them with my camera. Unfortunately, I couldn't get away, the gates were locked tight, I was doomed!

Georgina Beeson (12)

The Tailor's Dummy

She'd heard stories. Stories that could paralyse the human mind with a feeble whisper. Unfortunately, she ignored them. So they dared her. It was on that day that she made the biggest mistake of her life; she accepted.

The hefty door slammed behind her shutting out the nonsensical jeering and forcing her to focus on the bare wooden floorboards. She noticed nothing in the dank, lifeless room but a mirror smothered in dirty, smudged fingerprints and deep scratches engraved in the brass frame. About to look away, she spied a figure running quickly past in the reflection and a light flickered on in the corner.

Out of the dimness shone a tailor's dummy. An oddly deformed tailor's dummy, with a deep crimson velvet curtain covering the top …

Her heart began to beat harder and thump in her chest, breaking the screeching silence and a small, thin, very bony hand with small, thin, very bony fingers ripped off the curtain. There, impaled on the spike of the dummy, was an exact replica of her head, bleeding from the eyes …

Gemma Barnes (13)

The Garage

Twelve nights! Twelve sleepless nights of hammers and nails from next door. What they were doing in that garage, the man, who'd only just moved in, didn't know. He didn't know and he didn't care. All he could concentrate on was *undoing* it. Who would dare wake him? *He* deserved his rest.

Twelve nights! Twelve sleepless nights of hammers and nails. That's how long it'd taken me to fix the garage door. I don't know how it broke really. It couldn't have been vandals, because I'm miles from anywhere.

As I stood bolting it in, I swore I could hear someone crunching the driveway gravel, but no one was to be seen as I peered through the window, just my car with its frosted up windscreen. *Crunch.* Nothing? *Crunch.* Still nothing. *Crunch. Crunch.* A chill was sent down my spine and a shiver sank through my skin. I had to get out. All I knew was that I *had* to get out. I scrambled over to the towering steel door, opened it and tried to run out. But I couldn't. Something was stopping me. Some invisible force as strong as a brick wall was blocking my way. Like the Titanic I sank to my knees, scratching and pushing at the air. All the time a *crunch, crunch, crunch* ringing in my ears.

Armed with a basebell bat the man walked down the driveway and towards the building. He stepped through the door and went inside.

It was at this point that he became visible to me. I saw him the very instant he stepped onto the concrete floor. Tall, he stood before me, as I rose from my knees. He had unkempt, brown hair and pale, translucent skin. There was a distant look in his cold, grey eyes that I couldn't quite place.

'Oh hello,' he said as if surprised to see me.

I was convinced that he was hiding something behind his back.

'I just moved in next door and was wondering whether I could . . . borrow some . . . ?'

'Sugar?' I finished his sentence for him. How silly I had been! He must have been behind the car when I looked out of the window.

He started to look awkward and shifty. 'I've erm . . . got to go,' he announced nervously. Mumbling something about the time, he took a step back. He walked out. I blinked and he was gone.

There have been a few more visitors from our neighbours recently. All coming in through the garage. It's only now that I think about it, that I realise I must have misheard that man. There is no next door. Just a plot of land. The cemetery.

Peter Humphreys (13)

Kitty Cat Attack!

One day when I went to school I saw a cat in the middle of the road. I walked over to it to stroke it and it bit me. I walked away to look at my cut, the cat was gone when I looked back.

I went to school and forgot about the cat. But when I was on the way home there were two cats. When I got closer my finger was really hurting. I stared at my finger in surprise. The scar was shaped in writing, it said, *'you're dead'.*

That night I had a dream. It was about me turning into a cat. It was so realistic.

When I got out of bed that morning I saw four pairs of eyes looking at me from the corner of my room. Then I lifted my leg up and with my foot scratched behind my ear . . . *my ear!*

Alfie Gill (11)

The Necklace

Alice sprinted down the stairs at top speed, the pearly-white figure gliding metres behind. As she reached the bottom, she chanced a glance behind her, the ghost had gone. She turned to the hall to see the poltergeist standing directly in front of her, the transparent face inches from her own. Alice screamed and tore towards the front door into the garden. She stopped and clutched the stitch at her side, panting and looking around for the ghostly girl. She was hoping, praying, that this was just a dream, her imagination. She pinched herself; it hurt, she was awake.

She backed into the sundial, silent tears rolling down her cheeks. She froze in terror as an arm shot out of the sundial and grabbed her, closely followed by the rest of the spirit girl. Alice screamed and struggled against the girl, 'Get off me!' she begged.

'You have something of mine,' the ghost spoke in a high, rippling voice which made Alice's hair stand on end.

'I don't have anything of anyone's,' she replied desperately, still struggling against the girl's grip.

The girl said, 'The necklace, give it to me.'

Alice took off her necklace; she'd do anything to get rid of the girl, she held it out to the transparent being. The girl took it, there was a strong wind, the moon was blocked out and Alice could see nothing but darkness. Then the wind lifted and the moon reappeared, the spirit of the girl had gone.

Nicolle Hockin (12)

El Faba's Ghost

'He walks with a cane and he's always got a black cloak on. His name is El Faba, or rather it was!' Izzie said in low tones. 'He wears a mask all the time and it only shows his blood-red eyes, a gun bulges in his pocket.'

'And ...' Sandra continued in an awful voice.

'He only murders teenage girls, like us!'

'Stop it, you're making this all up,' shrieked Felicity, twiddling her thumbs.

'No we're not, Sarah Hamri told us last week, he's a really freaky ghost isn't he? Anyway, he has short black hair and he always either shoots his victims or he throttles them with his cane,' Sandra was whispering now.

'Yeah, and when he talks to his victims,' Marian went on sounding scared, 'he always hugs them and speaks to them softly and lovingly.'

'And imagine,' Izzie said spookily, 'if he came to the door right now.'

Ding-dong!

All the other girls shivered.

'With his cloak,' Izzie carried on spooking them, 'he wears jeans, a T-shirt and trainers.'

They carried on watching the scary movie they had been watching until the doorbell rang.

They went to the door together and opened it to see a young man in a T-shirt, jeans and trainers. Something bulged in his pocket and he had a black mask and cloak. He had short black hair and was wearing sunglasses over his red eyes. It was the ghost of El Faba. The girls screamed in unison … !

Eleanor Dumbill (11)

Murder Story

The rain splattered down upon the dark, deserted street. A silver Mercedes rolled past, spraying Charles with filthy rainwater, soaking him through to the bone. Charles was a small journalist, working on a local newspaper, 'The Express and Star'. He was making his way home, walking more quickly than usual to get out of the rain. He then became aware of a shape gliding behind him. He spun around, but only to find that whatever had been there had disappeared. He carried on, telling himself that he was imagining things. He hadn't seen anything, had he?

He quickened his pace even more now, wishing to get back home. He turned down a side alley which was a useful short cut. But halfway down he realised something was wrong. He stopped now, unaware of the rain pounding on the floor. He slowly turned around and his insides froze. A ghost - no, the Grim Reaper, was following him. It carried a giant scythe and wore a monk's habit. Charles couldn't see its face, the darkness surrounded it. Charles couldn't move, his legs were frozen to the ground in fear. Then it disappeared. Charles screamed and turned round. It was there again, scythe raised. It bought it down sharply with a sickening thud.

If Charles had still been alive, this would have been his best murder story yet.

Oliver Hunt (13)

Her Face Still Haunts My Dreams

I will never forget that day, 16th December 2000. A few days before Christmas. The weather was still and frost blanketed the streets. I left my house as usual and got into my silver BMW. I slid out of the driveway and eased along the A27, the usual way to work, but this was no ordinary day.

I was 21 then and zooming up the ladder to success, my own home, my wife. I was to be a father. As I turned into Newport my terror began.

There, standing on the pavement, was a girl about seven years old. Small and dressed in a green and yellow school uniform. She stepped into the road. She didn't see me. My engine was too quiet. Panic struck me. I braked. She hit the bonnet and her broken face careered into my windscreen. Her lifeless eyes gazed into mine, but I knew they couldn't see.

I screamed. I looked away in horror, cursing her stupidity, cursing my brakes. I opened my tear-filled eyes expecting to see those poor, hideous pupils. But she wasn't there. I felt joy at first, but then fear. How could she be alive? Her face had been less than a foot from mine; it was cold, lifeless, dead.

My car was unscratched and not a drop of blood was ever found. No accident was ever reported. But her face still haunts my dreams.

Tom King (13)

The Traveller

A toasty warm log fire was burning in the corner of the pub. The traveller who had entered a few hours ago sat in the corner swigging at a pint of beer as all fell silent, ready to hear his story:

'It was around nine that I left the gas station and by about one in the morning I noticed something wrong with my bike. So I stopped. It was a warm night, like most in the desert. I got out my tool kit and got to work fixing the carburettor.'

By now silence had fallen in the pub and everyone was listening eagerly to the stranger's story.

'As I lay down to rest I noticed something. The stars in the sky were going off … um … kind of like a Christmas tree. I felt something out there, something evil. Suddenly I noticed something around me.'

The bartender passed him another pint which he downed in one gulp and wiped his moustache before continuing. 'In a perfect circle around me there was a black tunnel of smoke forming, coming from nowhere. I somehow knew that if it closed in on top of me, then I was a goner.'

He motioned for the bartender to pass him another drink, which he reluctantly did. 'I fumbled in my bag, desperately searching for my Webley pistol. I knew, somehow, that the light would make this … this evil go away. I made a snap decision.' He looked around the bar slowly. 'I wired up the headlight on my bike and shone it straight through the smoke. And that's when I saw it.'

The pub was so quiet that you could hear a pin drop.

'In this 'smoke' I saw a face, no not a face, a skull. It was staring at me with its empty sockets. Then I realised the smoke was declining, falling back into itself or dying, if you will.'

The men in the bar stared. They could not believe their eyes, but they weren't staring at the newcomer. Something was taking shape in the smoke of the log fire …

Ralph Butler (13)

The Ghost On The Bridge

It was late, about quarter-past midnight; the street was silent bar the noises booming from within the pub. It was a very unsuspecting night, the moon just shone dimly onto the streets. The pub was about half full and a man, quite drunk, but not completely senseless, stumbled out of the pub. He was to walk home, down over the bridge, through a few more streets and home he would be. It was no normal night, this night however …

One hundred years to that day, that hour, that minute, just as this man was crossing the bridge, a man had been murdered. This man was drunk and coming from the same pub. He had had a brawl earlier with a person, a man from over the road from where he lived. A big brawl, the drunk had come off better then, but …

It was now about ten to midnight, the man was on the bridge walking, a rustle could be heard in a nearby bush. He stopped, he was sweating strangely …

The drunk heard a rustle too, but the result wasn't prolonged. His 'friend' from over the road jumped out and strangled him. He left him there to be scavenged by the foxes.

He stood still, a strange white glow was appearing around his neck and it formed into the shape of some hands. They squeezed harder; he had died. The wind whispered through the air the five words, '*I have had my revenge*'. For the great grandson of the man who killed someone on the bridge, one hundred years ago had died.

Petar Besevic (13)

The Neat Freak Ghost

'So son, what do you think?' questioned Jane.

'Pretty big, eh Jack?' added Peter.

'Yeah, it looks great.'

Jane, Peter and Jack had arrived at their new home, 'The Broadside' in Woodseaves, the biggest forest in Britain. There wasn't a house for miles, you know why? Because everybody in this area had been killed off by the Neat Freak Ghost.

It was now 8pm and getting dark.

'Jack! Peter and I are going to town, are you coming?'

'No, I am going to explore.'

He went straight to the swing in his garden where he went backwards and forwards. Then the shed mysteriously opened and a lawnmower jumped out and violently started raging around the garden. Jack, petrified, dashed to the back door that queerly opened for him as he sprinted to his bedroom and tripped over his bag. Clothes fell out, but were automatically folded back up. Now screaming, Jack ran to the forest and pounced under a tree panting for breath. He heard cracks . . . *thud* . . . the tree had fallen down . . . he was dead!

'And today's top story on Central News, last night in Woodseaves the Neat Freak Ghost struck again, killing three victims. They were new to the forest with a child being found dead under a tree and two adults dead in a Mercedes. How long until the ghost kills its 307th victim?'

Jacob Williamson (12)

The Phone Call

A low mist hangs over the cobbled driveway. An icy wind howls mournfully. It is eight o'clock in the morning, but it is light. The shutters bang and somewhere in the depths of the house a door creaks slowly shut.

Suddenly, there is a knock on the door. James opens the door of his new home. The sight that greets him shocks him; he feels a cold hand grasp his heart as it tries to escape and cower in his throat.

A tall imposing figure looms in the doorway, he is dressed in a worn black traveller's cloak. His face is hideously disfigured and there is a gaping abyss where his nose should be. A pair of dark sunglasses hide his eyes. 'Please may I use your phone? It is very urgent,' he asks politely in a strong German accent.

James tears his eyes away from the man's face. 'Yes, of course, please come in,' he finds his lips saying independently from the rest of his body, which is screaming at him to refuse.

James guides him to the ancient telephone.

The man's voice speaks out of the shadows, James starts, he has not heard the door open.

'I must go now,' the man whispers mysteriously.

James watches him fade into the mist, a solitary ghost.

Later James discovers that a German businessman had died nearby at six o'clock. Yet his wife had received a chilling phone call two hours later, saying he loved her and would be seeing her soon …

Ed Warren (13)

Captain Bill

Steve felt relaxed by the sound of the powerful waves crashing against the hard coastal rock. He always felt like this, he felt like he was truly alone, like no one was watching him, like he had no expectations to fulfil.

He had come here to get away from home, to leave all his troubles behind him, to forget about the fight he had just had with his over-protective father. They had got in a fight over nothing as usual and Steve had stormed out swearing that he wouldn't come back until his dad promised to make some changes and unfortunately he had just dismissed it as an idle threat.

Steve's feelings of tranquillity and peace were abruptly stopped by a cry that rang out along the shoreline. 'Cap'n Bill sailed the seas time and time again!'

Steve looked out into the dark sea and noticed the unmistakable sails of a ship. Sure they were a bit torn, but they were definitely those of a ship.

The large ornate ship weighed anchor in a large cave not far from where Steve sat.

He was about to get on board the ship when he felt the cold iron of a pistol barrel press into the back of his head. He began to turn around, but before he had a chance he heard a click then a bang and then nothing.

Now he wouldn't be going home, even if his dad did change.

Iain Hockin (13)

Long Time Dead

Natasha's heart gave a single, echoing beat of joy. A letter for her. She knew from the moment she saw it what it was. She eagerly knifed through the flimsy packaging like a woman possessed and her eyes blazed like celebratory bonfires.

Finally, Saturday came. Natasha, attired with thick black sludge, impaling jewellery and a desire that could wait no longer, embarked upon a noble and exciting crusade of darkness. She had won the competition of a lifetime. Little did she know, it would soon end a lifetime …

The atmosphere was toxic. The light was fading into darkness and hundreds of thousands of sweating, pulsing humans were reciprocating up and down, whilst the notorious riffs of 'Long time dead', filled the air. As they trudged off the stage adorned in masks and rags to gratuitous applause and shrieks of praise, Natasha waited backstage like a panther, with baited breath.

Her heart exploded. She was waiting impatiently outside the dressing room of 'Long Time Dead'. Timidly, like an anxious animal on death's doorstep, she knocked three times. Nobody had come to meet her, she found it strange. It was like the band weren't real. She entered the dark abyss alone and surveyed the nine masked men. She heard one of the men whisper, 'Congratulations, we are Long Time Dead.'

Suddenly, Natasha's body jerked and she fell to the floor. She just had enough strength to hear one man say, 'Welcome to our newest member …'

Tom Overmire (13)

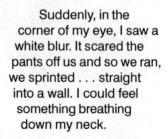

A Tale Of One Sheep, Dead Or Alive

That fateful day began with breakfast, crunchy nut cornflakes with ice-cold milk. It was an uneventful day, but not so in the cold, misty night.

We should never have gone in there, the house that the old fogies always used to say was haunted. The black and white one with lions at the gates guarding the house from the howling gale.

We were twelve then, and it was one o'clock in the morning. We had ventured outside after dark and drunk a can of Carling each. We thought we were really drunk. Maybe that was why Mikey suggested we went.

Berrington Kennels, our prized playground, was supposed to have been built on an old pet cemetery, where a mad old person buried his dog Scruffy, after he had died. If this was true, well we didn't even think about it.

The plan was just to leave a dead mouse my cat had caught the other day on the doorstep. We never meant to go in, but we did. It was meant to be a great prank, but it wasn't.

We ventured inside, with just a creak of a floorboard, but instantly I felt uneasy.

Suddenly, in the corner of my eye, I saw a white blur. It scared the pants off us and so we ran, we sprinted . . . straight into a wall. I could feel something breathing down my neck.

'God help us . . . '

A living sheep. But when did it live?

Matthew Saull (12)

Deadsville Mansion Sleepover

It was Friday night and Beth, Allie and Sophie were having a sleepover. They were in the middle of a game of dares when Sophie had an idea.

'What about if we go up to the Deadsville Mansion for the sleepover?' asked Sophie.

'But isn't that place meant to be haunted?'

'No, it isn't, that's just a legend,' exclaimed Beth, 'it's not true.'

'OK then, let's go,' said Allie.

The girls arrived at the mansion. As they went through the gates they looked at each other. 'Are you sure it's only a legend?' asked Allie.

Once inside the girls looked around for the best place to sleep, each door creaked as it opened. Suddenly they heard a noise from the basement, they opened the door and put on the light and looked down the stairs, slowly they climbed down. Sophie stumbled and fell. She knocked over a box and behind it she found a half-opened coffin with a bony arm sticking out. The girls ran screaming and shouting.

The front and back doors were locked, so they went up to the attic to get out of the window. They pushed their way through cobwebs; Beth was just about to smash the window when Allie screamed.

'What is it?' asked Beth.

'C-c-coffin!' gasped Allie.

All the coffins were named. The first coffin said, 'Allie Dyer'. The second coffin said, 'Sophie Baker'. The third coffin said, 'Beth Taylor'.

There was a noise. Then another and another.

Samantha Jones (10)

The Black Hounds

Mack and Cary were bored, they'd been in the car for three hours and twenty-five minutes, Mack had been counting.

'Where's the new house?' asked Cary.

'In the middle of the wood,' replied Mum.

'How much did it cost?' asked Cary.

'Five pounds,' replied Dad happily.

Cary had been asking that every ten minutes.

'We're here,' Mum sighed, and the car stopped, slowly.

Mack and Cary dashed into the new, wooden, creaky house. It was very big and for some reason it made Mack's tummy churn as he looked around it.

'Wow!' exclaimed Mum. 'Is it night-time already? Who's up for their first night in the new house?'

Nobody answered, except for Dad.

Mack couldn't get to sleep. He tossed and turned and looked all around the room until he decided to have a drink. He snuck down the stairs, but they creaked and when he was in the kitchen, he had a horrible feeling he was being watched, so he backed his way upstairs.

He had only just got back into bed when there was a crash downstairs; the whole family woke up.

There was something trying to get in.

'Quick Dad, we've got to get to the car!' shouted Cary.

They rushed to the door when they heard a howl from the living room. They ran straight out of the house, but Mack saw some glistening eyes turn to him.

Everything was quiet, everyone was scared when suddenly something jumped onto the car making it rumble. A giant black dog was trying to get into the car through the sunroof!

'Dad, you left the sunroof open!' yelled Mack.

Another dog was trying to topple the car over from the side.

'Well this is the end!' wailed Mum.

And then the sun came up, the dogs panicked. They ran all over the place, but when the sun hit them they turned to stone. The family left after that, but not before throwing the dog statues into the river, where they sank to the bottom.

Dino Carobene (10)

House Of Doom

One day Luke was walking in the countryside. It soon got dark and he became lost.

It started to rain. He found a big old house in the trees. Luke knocked on the door, there was so reply. He knocked again and the door opened, but there was nobody there. 'Hello, is anybody there?' Luke shouted. So Luke went in.

Luke looked around the house, it was damp and cold but it was pouring with rain so he thought he would spend the night there.

Later that night the wind howled like ten wolves. Suddenly Luke heard a very loud noise, like a gun firing. Luke looked around. He rushed out of the door and saw a light on in the other room. He saw two transparent people hovering and talking about how they were going to get him out of the house.

Luke was shaking with fright, he grabbed his bags and ran out of the house. The ghosts now behind him, screaming, 'Never come back here again.' He heard them still screaming as he ran all the way home.

Matthew Flook (10)

Portsdown

Captain John Miller of the yacht Portsdown was worried. He was near Southampton and since he had left, this accursed fog had fallen. Well, he had better get back there. He called to the crew, 'Check the compass.' The answer was not to his satisfaction. The compass was broken. The needle danced lightly around the disc, pointing at random. He swore. 'Right, send out an SOS.'

Five minutes later, the radio operator stuck his head out of the hatch. 'It's all gone Sir, all static.'

John stared out into the dense white mist. There was the bulk of the Isle of Wight, strangely comforting. Then something else loomed up, a steamer. He yanked on the foghorn rope. Nothing happened. The steamer continued, then there was a blinding flash and a great bang. The steamer's bow was blasted out of the water. Or was it? It had a very strange white texture. Come to think of it, he wasn't even so sure it was a steamer at all. It had more the texture of fog. Then the mist swirled away and there was only one big empty expanse of The Solent, where a few small sailing yachts plied the calm water.

Kit Freiesleben (11)

The Owen's Field Underpass Hauntings

It was the old demountables with the creaky stairs that set the whole thing off. It was a hot summer's day and school was getting too much for Samantha Rhyley. She slipped out at lunchtime to Owen's field underpass. This was named after Rudolph Owen who died, birdwatching in the field. Samantha jumped as high as she could in an attempt to reach the ceiling but just missed. She tried again and again until she got it. As soon as her hand touched the roof, a rope tightened around her neck and she heard the distinctive laugh of Rudolph Owen. On the descent, the rope hanged her. When an old man found her the following day, there was no sign of a rope or a strangling, she was just lying there as dead as a rock.

So when I was with friends in Priorslee, I thought I might dare them to go down there and see what was there. I haven't slept a wink since. We went down there together. When we got there, we just froze. What we saw was horrible, white and translucent, she was just hanging there with a rope attached to nothing. We turned. We ran and didn't stop running until we were safe at home. We thought. We turned on the television and to our horror, saw Samantha Rhyley staring at us with a blank expression on her face.

That face has haunted our dreams ever since.

Robert Ogden (13)

Midnight Hanging

Midnight. Black, dreary, dark … haunted.

The man stumbled along the forest path, cursing aloud those who had thrown him out of his home. Tired and aching, he had even forgotten the reason for his banishment … but of course; the girl. He had murdered her. But she had laughed at him, surely that was cause enough! Through his crazed, bloodshot eyes he looked up at the sky, the rain falling around him, and howled like a wild beast. The thunder echoed in reply. He continued on, falling to his knees and crawling like a dog.

And then he saw her, or at least it seemed to be her. It was the girl, a figure made of smoke, floating above the ground, always ahead of him, always laughing. He was gripped in a mad fury; she had had him sent away! It was her fault! Everything was!

He ran towards her, his hands stretching for her. She must die, properly this time! But she was still ahead of him, still laughing. And in his blind rage he did not notice the noose, hanging from a branch where she had placed it; a trap. She had gone straight through it, but it went round his neck and tightened. He could not escape. He dropped like a stone. She laughed for the last time and left, she had had her revenge.

You can still hear his screams.

Jospeh Peplinski (13)

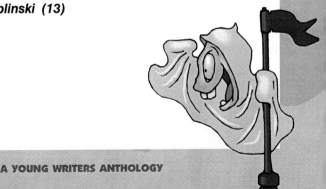

Hello Again Mr Hiller

Fleeting visions of the last time this had happened crossed Jim Collins' mind. The giddy feeling, the same as you get on really fast roller coaster rides as he had tripped over the loose engine cable and toppled headfirst over the edge of the Lincoln RF398 bomber. Then the sickly crunch of bone on stone as he collided with the floor 20 feet below, and finally the white wisp of vapour that shrouded him, gathered him close and whispered in his ear.

'You have saved my plane, Mr Hiller is grateful.'

It's that time again, but this time I'm a gonner, he thought to himself as he plummeted earthward. He closed his eyes and prayed to the Lord to be spared when, *hey! It's taking a ruddy long time to hit the ground here.* He opened his eyes again and fell the extra two feet onto the floor. People came running from all the doors checking what all the commotion was.

'Are you all right, Jim?' asked Bob.

'Yeah, I'm fine,' he replied, but suddenly his blood ran cold as a voice in his ear said …

'Thank you soldier, Mr Hiller is grateful.'

Rhys Davenport (13)

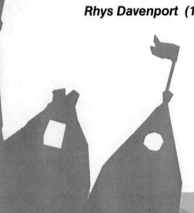

The Witch Hunter

It was the middle of the night on the evening before Hallowe'en, and the Macclesfield family were all snug in their beds, in their Edwardian house in Suffolk. James was having a particularly good dream until a cold, blue, burning torch landed on his lap. He awoke because of a cold breeze on his cheek. When he saw the flame he screamed. As the rest of the Macclesfield family came, they heard a ghostly shriek come echoing down the hall. Rushing past the bedroom door came a translucent man in his nightclothes, beckoning for his family who weren't far behind.

The Macclesfields followed the mystery family down the stairs and into the kitchen, where a butler and a chef were being attacked by a horde of ghostly vagrants, who butchered them in the middle of the kitchen floor. More vagrants came through the closed door and took the father of the ghost family away. Flames poured down the stairs. As the Macclesfields took cover behind the kitchen counter, Sarah found a diary with 'I fear for my life …' on the last page. She looked over the cover of the book to find that she was sitting in burnt out rubble in the middle of a field, for the house was also a ghost, after having been burnt down. This was the house of the legendary Matthew Hopkins, the Witch Hunter General, who was killed by a band of peasants believing he was a warlock.

Michael Brown (13)

Down The Long, Muddy Track

As we drove down the long, muddy track, the trees began to engulf the light of the sun. The leafless trees darkened the woodland. As we approached the hidden palace, we saw the door begin to open. My younger brother had been left alone for the past hour. Once we had got out of the car, a cold chill swooped past, slamming the front door and some windows above that we had not noticed previously. As we cautiously entered through the only door, the cold breeze became colder. In the corner of the hallway was a breathing mass, which carried the tears of fear. My mother attended him while I searched around.

As I entered the dining hall I noticed the fire was lit, which helped bring light to the dim candles. As I exited, I noticed something. A white wisp passed through a crack in the ceiling into the room. I looked through the keyhole and watched as one by one, this figure threw my dad's paintings into the flames. And every time one went in, my brother's tears grew louder.

I noticed the fire start to settle and could no longer see the white figure. Suddenly a white translucent eye came face to face with me in the keyhole. I felt dizzy.

I ran to my mother to tell her what I had seen. I didn't hear her, but it looked like she was screaming at me. As though she had seen a ghost!

Robert Pike (13)

The Ghost Of Scariville

Ten o'clock. It was the end of John's working hours at the hospital and he was on his way home. But, little did he know what was happening that night. He left the car park and drove down most of the country lanes leading to his home. But then, the street lights went off. John had no idea where he was going and he was on an icy road. After a while he ran out of petrol and was sliding down off a cliff to his death. Somehow the car stopped right at the edge of the cliff. Spectres and zombies were standing on the edge pushing the car back up. But then, the zombies jumped into the car and set it on fire. Three hours later he was home after walking five miles and stopping for a rest. He was unaware of the past that was gaining on his future.

When he was at home he went upstairs and the electrics started fluctuating. Strange, face-like shadows were appearing around the room. He was stuck upstairs and ghosts were appearing in the exact spot where his wife was murdered. His past was catching up. Then, thunder struck and lightning quickly followed. He fled into the attic.

Then, the attic door closed and locked almost instantly. All the ghosts were gone, all but one, which left a bloodstain on the spot where John had murdered his wife at 2am. He has remembered this ever since, and every Hallowe'en the ghost 'returns'.

Jack Lovatt (13)

The Girl That Disappeared

'Jenny! You're falling to sleep again,' moaned Mrs Brown.

'What, where am I?' a confused Jenny said.

'You really must have an early night today, you're not concentrating anymore.'

'Yes, Mrs Brown.'

After tea that night, following her teacher's advice, she headed upstairs to bed. She collapsed onto her bed and soon after, she was in a relaxing sleep.

'Jenny!' a droning voice moaned. 'Jenny,' it said again.

'Who's that?' she said, jumping up from her bed.

'Commme tooo meeee,' the voice moaned.

She walked across to her window. High in the clouds, the moon was being chased by the night, dodging among the clouds and then disappeared. Looking down into the garden, an unwelcome shape was moving!

Running down the stairs, through the kitchen she ran and then she opened the door.

On top of a horse sat a huge hooded man. 'I've been waiting for you …'

Gavin Kelleher (10)

The Locket

Lucy was an only child who lived with her dad. When Lucy was three, her mum had passed away. Lucy had nothing to remember her mum by, except some soppy photos of her and Dad, and a few crumpled ones of Lucy when she was a baby in her mum's arms, and a locket made of silver. Inside was a picture of her mum, and on the other side, her dad.

One night Lucy awoke, everything was pitch-black. Lucy could not hear a thing except her dad snoring, and a strange noise downstairs. Lucy went down, thinking her dad might have left the telly on by accident. As she got to the last step, she heard a strange noise coming from the lounge, but the telly was off! She turned, only to see …

'Why, why?' she shrieked, her pale face so white you could call her a ghost! She was.

'Why, what?' Lucy shrieked.

'I have been dead for eight years. Why me, why not you?' her voice was like ice. 'Just give me the locket!'

Lucy took it off her neck. A flash of blue light and the pale face of her mum was gone, and so was her locket!

Hattie Ellis (10)

The Misty Manor House

It was the first day of the summer holiday. Tom always had a lie-in on the first day of the summer holiday because they always went on holiday the first night. Tom couldn't wait.

'Tom, have you packed your stuff yet?' shouted Mum up the stairs.

Tom loved going on holiday, even though he's a scaredy-cat, especially at night. The time soon came.

'Is everyone in the car?' asked Dad.

They set off on their adventure. They were almost there when they turned into a dark, misty, spooky lane that led them to the Old Manor House where they were staying the weekend. The wind was howling through the lane.

'Argh!' screamed Tom.

Dad slammed his brakes on after something dived in front of the car. Silence hit the car, except for Mum shaking and shivering. Everyone was still, like they'd been frozen.

'Whatever it was has gone into the dark, gloomy woods,' said Tom.

They carried on going, the wind picked up. They soon arrived at the Old Manor.

Dad opened the door, it creaked open.

'Yuck, look at that on the wall,' whispered Tom.

Blood was smeared all over. A shiver went down Mum's back. They then went upstairs, noises were everywhere. Tom opened a cupboard, a mouldy skeleton fell out and hit him on the head!

'Bedtime!' shouted Dad.

Everyone jumped into bed. The wind was still howling and Mum was still shaking.

'What was that?' shrieked Tom, in a scared voice.

Mum sat up and turned the light on, a rat scuttled along the floorboards. It was like it was haunted. They couldn't wait until breakfast.

They all rushed downstairs in the morning. Yum-yum, it was porridge for breakfast.

Suddenly as they started tucking in, a groan came from a gentleman in the left-hand corner. He had been stabbed, blood shot everywhere and his face landed in the porridge.

They all ran upstairs and packed their stuff and sped off down the lane. They could not wait to get away from the Haunted Manor. Suddenly, Dad shouted, *'Look!'*

They must have missed the sign which read - *Murder Mystery Weekend.*

Tom Edwards (10)

The Ghost Hunter

There was an old, spooky house with ivy overgrowing the windows, so nobody could see what was going on in there. Nobody lived there, but people say that it's haunted. A lady called Mrs Macready said that she saw three ghosts in there, and their names were Ronnie (a bus driver), Tess (a fashion designer) and Jordan (the shoe-shine boy). They were friendly ghosts, but there was one problem, the ghost hunters! They hunt the ghosts and put them in jars and kill them. The ghost hunters names were Mrs Disnif and Mr Disnif.

'Can we go out tonight?' said Jordan.

'No we can't, we've got ghost school,' replied Ronnie.

'Well I can't go because I'm polishing my nails!' said Tess.

'You are coming to ghost school with me, Tess!' Ronnie replied angrily.

'Oh, all right, but I have to do my nails first,' she replied.

'Well, I'm going out right now!' Jordan said, as he rushed out of the door.

'Wow, what's the matter with him?' said Tess and Ronnie.

'Ronnie, let's look at our camera to see what's going on outside,' she said.

'OK,' he replied.

'Look! Look! There's Jordan,' Tess said excitedly.

'Yes, but look who's behind him,' Ronnie said.

'Argh! The ghost hunters!' Tess screamed.

Ronnie and Tess were very worried!

'Quick, we need to save Jordan,' Ronnie screamed.

'Yes, and quick!' she panicked.

But when the two ghosts got down there, the ghost hunters had already put him in a jar.

'Ronnie, we need to save him,' screamed Tess.

'OK, follow those ghost hunters!' said Ronnie.

They followed the ghost hunters into a little black cave, trying not to be seen.

'OK Tess, listen to me, this is what we're going to do,' ordered Ronnie.

The two ghosts made up a plan.

'Right Tess, you go right and I'll go left,' Ronnie said.

'OK,' Tess replied.

'Now, we both have to grab the jar and run for it, OK,' Ronnie said.

'OK!' Tess replied.

'One, two, three, grab the jar,' said Ronnie.

'Run for it!' said Tess.

Luckily they were not heard by the ghost hunters, or they would have been caught by the ghost hunters and put in a jar too!

The ghosts are safe at home now. They are back to normal and hopefully won't be bothered by the ghost hunters for a while. The ghosts don't mind if the ghost hunters come next time because they're going to be ready for them, aren't you ghosts?

'Yes!' they reply.

Grace Haines (10)

On The Night Of Hallowe'en

'Trick or treat?' called the three children.

Vicky, Sammy and Jack were all trick or treating on Hallowe'en. Vicky, who was the oldest, was dressed as a devil. Little Sammy, who was Vicky's little sister, was dressed up as a cat. Vicky, Sammy and Jack, their brother, who was waiting for them at their neighbour's gate, Sammy's face paint was as black as a cat, well she was a cat.

As they got to the end of their road, they began to go home. They took a short cut through the graveyard.

'Hurry up, Sammy, stop munching and walk faster, I've got a Hallowe'en party to go to,' called Vicky across a grave.

'Who's making that horrible racket?' called a voice.

It was a ghost, but not just any ghost. The three children had bad memories. Two years ago, a spirit told the children to kill a ghost, (to be ghost hunters). The children managed to kill the ghost, but the ghost's brother was back to haunt them.

'Come here,' one of the ghosts said to little Sammy, but she stayed put. Not for long. The ghost grabbed her again, this time she was stuck. The other two ghosts grabbed Jack and Vicky.

'Let them go,' a black cat screeched from behind Vicky. *'Run!'* the black cat yelled.

The three children and the cat all ran back to Vicky, Jack and Sammy's house.

Twenty minutes later …

The cat and children got back home within twenty minutes. The bad part was the ghosts knew where they lived. Jack opened the door to find three ghosts in front of them, standing like statues in the doorway. Vicky and Jack both ran down to the basement, all the ghosts followed them. But Sammy had a plan, she waited until they had all gone downstairs and she ran like a cheetah up to her bedroom. She rummaged in the cupboards, pulling out a grassy green gun with two nozzles coming out. She may only be seven, but she sure knows how to kill a ghost! Sammy hid behind the door until the ghosts came up.

'Where is that little brat?' they all asked.

Sammy dived out from behind the door and shot the gun. And with that, a fire-red blob shot out from the grassy green gun like lightning. The ghosts melted into goo, which Sammy refilled her gun with. She added a secret ingredient, we will never know exactly what it was.

Abby Hoyle (10)

The Witching Hour

The clock struck twelve. The witching hour had begun. Becky was at home on her own as her parents were at a dinner party. She was tucked up in bed when she was woken up by a banging. She blinked, opened her eyes, then sat bolt upright when she heard the sound again. She got up and went to her window and looked out. There was a storm, thunder was roaring and lightning was crashing. But that wasn't the only sound she'd heard.

She slowly made her way to the door then jumped at the banging again. She then made it onto the landing, frightened of what the noise was. Her sweaty palm grabbed the banister and she slowly started making her way down the stairs, with them creaking every step she took. As she was getting near the bottom, the banging was becoming louder. Shivers shot up her spine. The noise as coming from the living room and so she gradually made her way to the room. When she got there she tried turning on the light, but the power had gone. The slamming was now incredibly loud and it was coming from the window. All her hairs were standing on end, sweat running down her face. She took small, shuffling steps, her heart pounding in her chest as she edged towards the window. She then placed a firm grip on the curtain and pulled it open, letting out a piercing scream which echoed around the house.

Sasha Fever (14)

My Midnight Adventure

The sunset died down, a fearful shiver ran up my spine as the air balloon was taking me higher and higher into the dark and gloomy midnight sky. It was quite a spooky night, in winter as well, so it was very dark. It was really scary. No one around, all on my own, nowhere, no one to be seen. A flash ran past me, that's when I knew I wasn't alone.

It was cold, I was scared. It got spookier by the second. Another flash ran past me and something went through me, it was too spooky. I couldn't figure out what it was. I was too spooked out, I couldn't think what to do either. I heard a noise, but it didn't sound normal, and I knew I wasn't alone.

It grew darker and darker, as the noise got louder and louder, and the flash got brighter and brighter as it got spookier, then totally spooked out (that was me).

It was terrifying. I wasn't alone, but this thing wasn't normal. I was scared, I knew I wasn't safe outside alone. As the air balloon got higher, it grew darker. Silence is all that was around. The flash ran past me again, which made silence different. This thing went through me again and it had an evil laugh. That's when I knew it was a ghost. A flash ran past me, this time it was white. Knowing it was a ghost freaked me out even more.

The sunrise came out, blinding my eyes. I floated down in the air balloon to the morning of summer. I was still outside, but I knew I was safe because my friend came out and welcomed me. That's when I knew my midnight adventure was over.

Beth Newman (10)

The Haunted Mansion

'Tanya, I've got another house to redo, it's one of those mansions near the Pine Tree Wood, the one that's not been opened since 1954,' said Barry on his cell phone, leaving for work.

'I don't know what you are going on about,' answered Tanya.

'The one that no one ever goes into because it's said to be haunted,' informed Barry.

Baz had two kids, one called Gina, aged 12, Billy, aged 8, and a wife called Tanya, a housewife looking after the kids. Barry was the boss of a company called 'Bazzer's Window and Doors'.

Barry had to visit the mansion to find out the measurements for the windows. When he got there, there were so many windows and such big windows, that he didn't know if he would be able to get the measurements for every window. So he went back home and thought about what he was going to do.

That night, Barry and his workmates went out to a seafood restaurant. Baz didn't like seafood so he had a burger and chips, but his workmates all had seafood.

The next morning, Barry phoned up his mates to see if they could help him with the windows, but they were all ill from the seafood restaurant, so he asked his wife and kids if they would help him, but they wouldn't.

The day Barry had to go and measure the windows, the family were going to go on a family holiday camping down by a lake somewhere, with their canoe and fishing rods. So Barry asked them if they could stop on the way so he could get the measurements for the windows. So they loaded their car and hit the road. About half an hour later, they got to the house, got out of the car and walked across a bridge to the mansion.

'This place is really, really freaky,' said Billy, hiding behind Tanya's back.

'Ah, you scaredy-cat,' answered Gina.

'Stop it you two,' said Tanya angrily.

They walked up to the door and Baz opened it. They walked in …

The door closed straight behind them, they were trapped. Billy threw a stone at the window, but they were as solid as rock.

'You should never have come here, you will now suffer the consequences!' came a voice echoing out of the blue.

Then suddenly, a blinding light shone down, and then one minute later, Tanya and Gina were gone. The light had faded to nothing.

'Billy!' Barry shouted.

'Yeah, Dad?' answered Billy …

Billy and Barry ran up the stairs. As they were running, Barry felt something go through him. It was a ghost.

'Uh, buh, I, did I just go through you?' asked Barry speechlessly.

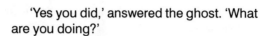

'Yes you did,' answered the ghost. 'What are you doing?'

'I'm looking for my wife,' answered Barry.

Then the ghost said, 'I can help you there, I know my way around this place like I know the back of my hand.'

Then they all walked up the creaky stairs. There were about twenty doors. They looked in every room, but they weren't in any of the rooms.

'There's just one door left,' said the ghost. He took a large painting off the wall, it was of a posh man in a suit, with a sword hanging off his belt, and a woman in a long white dress who looked like Tanya.

'Who's that woman in the picture?' asked Barry.

'That's Lady Isabella, and the man next to her is Sir Isaac O'Riley,' answered the ghost. 'She died long ago, and her soul still remains, he is probably going to join Lady Isabella's soul and your wife's body together, so he can get his wife back,' informed the ghost.

They ran to the door behind the picture, Barry knocked it down … There stood Sir Isaac O'Riley, holding a magic ball, whilst Tanya had been chained to a stone table. Gina was stirring a potion Tanya had to drink so the soul could join the body. Barry ran in and knocked the magic ball out of Sir Isaac O'Riley's hand, then it smashed to smithereens. Sir Isaac O'Riley had disappeared, then Lady Isabella's soul, and next the ghost who had helped Barry. Then things in the actual mansion disappeared, like the chains on Tanya and Gina, then the stone table.

'We've got to get out of here,' said Billy.

They all ran down the stairs as everything started disappearing. They ran out of the mansion and got into the car. Barry pulled out as fast as his car would go, then he went as fast as he could down the motorway and to the lake. Then suddenly, the mansion disappeared as Barry started to sing the song that was on the radio.

'Shut up Dad!'

Tom Payne (10)

Picture It

So there she stood, in the bathroom of his little house. The young girl needed to relieve herself before starting the proper pilgrimage. It was a dark room, for the guide had not even a lamp, he was so poor. She glanced up at the wall in front where there was a picture of several adults sitting round a fire in a field. They looked like trippers, especially one man in his fifties, near the front, who looked at the girl on the toilet hopefully, and …

Wait, she thought, *pictures do not turn to look at you.* Although once the girl had shaken herself out of her thoughts, the man in the picture had called over his wife (though dumbly to the girl doing her business) and they both stood smiling weakly and hopefully at her.

Hey, what is my imagination like? she thought to herself, and got off the toilet to look closely at the work of art on the wall. When the man in the front of the picture got on his knees in front of her eyes, she stumbled backwards, fell, and hit her head on the toilet pan. She was dead. A few minutes later, the old guide came in and saw her body on the floor, sighed and muttered, 'Gets 'em all.'

So next time you see a picture move, don't think your eyesight is going, remember this: *a picture is some poor person's soul, not a decoration.*

Jessica Leighton

Eternity

On a cold and dreary evening, James set out to have a walk around the neighbourhood. Most kids decided not to go out late, but he thought, *it can't be that bad.* He walked along the street. He could hear an owl hooting in the distance. The bitterly cold wind tore against his face. The trees formed disfigured shapes swaying to and fro. He started to get scared.

The wind suddenly threw a cold gust at him and beside him on the pavement was a dusty camera. James tentatively picked it up and examined it. It was an old camera, one of the type which you could change the lens. The camera was completely black and did not seem to be damaged, except for a small chip in the outer plastic. He put the camera to his eye and looked through; to his surprise the picture was absolutely clear. It was as clear as if he were looking out of an eye twice as powerful as his. James decided to take a photo. *Click, whirr.* A white figure leapt out. It was extremely disfigured, with its eyes bulging and its arms and legs all bent towards its body. It grabbed him and seemed to push him into the camera. He saw what seemed to be his ghost drifting out of him, but he wasn't inside that ghost. He stared out of the lens. He would have to look out of that lens for eternity, never closing his eyes.

Jeremy Brown (13)

Demons, Were They There?

I'm Abbey Simmons. I'm twelve now, so me and my mates, well, we took a spooky trip to this house in Poplar Close, and it was said to be haunted. We dared each other to go inside and take a look. We thought it would be fun and a good challenge. We walked up the crooked old steps. The door had a knocker with a face. As I looked more closely, it had a sparkle in its eye, as if it was real.

'Are you sure about this?' I gulped.

'You're not chickening out are you? You said you were a right daredevil,' they all giggled.

Well I showed them. I opened the door carefully and slowly. 'Well, are you coming?' I built up my courage finally. When we were all inside, the door *slammed* shut. We were scared so badly, we held hands, even the lads.

The sun shining through a tiny hole in the wall was the only bit of light downstairs. Sammy thought she'd try and be the brave one by stepping forward and was pushed back with force from … nothing. We all thought this was pretty weird. We pegged it upstairs. It was even darker up there, but there were a lot of candles about. Rhys and Danny had some matches. They lit them all up, it wasn't perfect but it was good enough. A dirty, old, cobweb-covered bookcase and a table were the only bits of existing furniture throughout the whole house.

Anna stepped forward and grabbed the nearest book out of the bookcase. The bookcase creaked open like a door; a pebbled path went through a yellow glow from the turrets on the wall. There were hovering demons, bloodstained walls. We started fighting, but they started biting, then there was nothing.

Abbey Simmons (12)

The Killer Doll

One day, a family moved into a house. The little girl found a doll and went to the dolls' shop and said, 'Can I swap the doll for a different doll?'

There were two sections. One of the sections was voodoo dolls, and the other section was cuddly toys. The little girl chose a voodoo doll, which was in the wrong section.

When she got home, she ran straight to her room and played with her toys. She didn't know that the doll she had picked was a voodoo doll. Every night she slept with the doll.

Then one night, the doll came alive at midnight and she sang this song as she walked up the stairs. 'I am on the first step, I am on the second step, I am on your mum's bed.' Then she stopped.

The next day, the mum was dead and the doll was missing a finger.

The next night, the doll did the same to her brother, and the doll was missing one more finger.

The rest of the family moved out and left the doll in the house, and never returned.

Roxanne Cover (11)

Ghost

Ella's school bus had just arrived at Red Bridge Camp, where Ella was staying. They put their luggage in their rooms. Ella's friend Laura was ill, so she couldn't come to camp, that meant Ella had a room to herself. It was OK, because Ella was only scared of ghosts, but she had never seen one before so she wasn't scared and she was next to the teacher's room. She thought she was safe.

'Hey, look what I've found,' shouted Ella.

She forgot she was orienteering in the fields. She found a small white ball with a black dot in the middle, with a green outline surrounding it.

That night she was not able to sleep because she heard weird noises coming from the hallway. She decided to go and have a look. Ella walked down the corridor and saw a door that she didn't see there earlier. It was half-open. Ella peered inside.

She tried not to scream, but she couldn't help it. 'Ghost!' screamed Ella.

The ghost heard her. The ghost turned around, he was wearing a purple robe, but he only had one eye. Ella realised the ball she had found was not a ball, it was his eye. She ran down the hallway and slammed the door.

'Ella, I'm at your door. Ella, I'm in your room. Ella, I'm on your bed. Ella ...' the ghost chanted.

'Aarrgghh!' screamed Ella.

The next morning, Ella was found hanging in her room.

Alex Robbins (10)

The Scariest Night Ever

In a dark room, two girls were sitting up in bed. They were just about to fall asleep when, *bang, boom, argh!* The room darted around, the lights flickered on, off, on, off, the trees rustled on the glass windows, then in one blink of an eyelash, everything went calm.

Sarah and Bethany were under the covers shaking like mad, as if they were at the North Pole.

'W-w-what was that?' said Sarah, in a very shaken up and frightened tone.

'I d-don't k-know,' said Bethany, who sounded like a mouse.

Sarah was just about to go to her mum, when she saw all her family dead on the floor. Sarah looked like a ghost.

When Beth took her eyes off her, she stared at the door. Then coming at her was a snake which was deadly, very! It hissed and spat, then it soared at Beth and bit her. Sarah suddenly fainted and Beth felt as sick as a dog and was seeing spots. She fell to the ground!

Sarah and Beth woke up. Was it a dream, or wasn't it?

'Aargh! I'm dead!'

Rebecca Brown (11)

Drip, Drip, Drip …

The old lady poured the cat food into the bowl. Yawning, she put it in the cat basket opposite her bed and then she fell asleep.

She awoke one hour later and heard a distant sound, *drip, drip, drip.*

Oh drat, she thought, *I must have left the tap on.* She heaved herself off her bed and made her way down the corridor into the bathroom. The tap wasn't dripping and the noise had stopped. *Weird!* she thought, and went back to bed.

Two hours later, she woke up once more and once again heard the noise, *drip, drip, drip.*

It must be the kitchen tap, she thought. She went downstairs and checked the tap. It wasn't on. The lady went upstairs thinking that she must be dreaming. Before she reached her bed, she looked over at the cat basket. Her cat wasn't there and the food was. 'Must be out hunting rats or something,' she muttered to herself.

At 2 o'clock, she woke up once more and for the third time she heard the sound. *Drip, drip, drip.* She was sure it was getting louder. 'It must be the shower!' she said out loud. She got up and walked to the bathroom. She pulled back her shower curtains and screamed. Her cat hung from a piece of rope, its insides on its outside, and blood dripping from it.

Before she could scream again, something grabbed her from behind and then she could scream no more …

Sabha Shahid (12)

The Birthday Ghost

I shivered in my pyjamas as the temperature dropped as fast as an elephant in a mouse cage. I slowly got out of bed and tiptoed out of my bedroom into the boiler room, but the heating was on.

Confused, I was about to get into my bed when I had the fright of my life. In my bed there was a thin, transparent ghost. While I was staring at him, the ghost held out a bony hand and he slowly opened it. Inside, there was a birthday card and a five pound note! Just as I was about to scream, I woke up in my bed at one minute past twelve, it was all a dream!

The next morning, while I was opening my birthday presents, there was a card containing a five pound note, saying, 'from your ghostly friend', but who was that … ?

John Light (12)

Ghost Story

Hi, I'm Elizabeth and I am going to tell you a ghost story. I'll start at the beginning in 1949. A happy girl called Ethel lived in a big house on the corner of a leafy street with her mum and dad. A year after they moved in, Ethel's mum died and shortly after, her dad married a lady called Maggie. She was horrible to Ethel.

Ethel knew that Maggie didn't love her dad. She had worked out why Maggie married him, it was the house and the money. Ethel's dad knew she wasn't happy, so he bought her a horse, a lovely grey mare.

One wild, stormy night, Ethel's dad suddenly died and soon after the funeral, Maggie went on holiday, leaving Ethel all alone. Ethel didn't like being alone and she let her horse sleep in her bedroom.

One night while they were asleep, there was a creak of the front door, the scrape of a match, and the house was ablaze. Ethel and the horse were killed. Maggie was caught and found guilty.

In 1998, a nice family moved into the renovated house. A year later, while they were asleep, a spark started a terrible fire. Neighing sounds and clattering of hooves woke the family. They said that a young girl and a ghostly grey mare led them through the smoke and flames to safety.

People say that the house is enchanted. Sometimes they see Ethel and her brave grey mare walking in the grounds.

Elizabeth Cottrell (10)

The House Of Ghosts

'I still don't see why we have to move!' Molly whined. 'I was fine here, at our old house.'

'We are moving because we have to, Molly,' Simon said. 'I know you're seven years old and you don't understand like me and Eddy do.'

'Just shut her up, Simon, and we can be on our way there. It's only a short walk away, so move it!' Eddy said impatiently.

'Eddy, don't yell!' Simon said. 'And just because I'm 12, Molly's seven and you're 15 doesn't mean you're the boss of us, now can we please go to the house!'

When they got there, Simon was about to knock, when the door creaked open by itself. 'That's strange,' Simon said and walked inside.

He looked at the hallway; there were suits of armour on stands leaning against the wall. Molly looked at one from behind Simon, who was looking at them all. The suit that Molly was looking at, Molly seemed to like. Then she saw the hand armour (where the knuckles were) slightly tighten its grip around the handle of its long sword.

She told her brothers about it. Eddy teased her, but Simon comforted her and half believed her, so Molly and Simon investigated the armour.

When they were examining it, it came to life and said, 'Who disturbs the living dead?'

It sounded like three voices speaking at once. Luckily, Simon had read about ghosts and their weaknesses, so he took the armour apart and the ghost fled.

Matt Archer (10)

My Ghost Story

There once lived a little girl, who lived in the countryside with her mum, her dad and her big sister. They were quite a quiet family, in fact, they hardly ever went out of their house. The little girl's name was Sarah. She'd been through a lot for her age. Firstly, her grandma had died, and now her dad had told her he and her mum were not her real parents and she'd been adopted.

That night when Sarah and her sister had gone to bed, they heard strange noises, but Sarah's sister being as old as she was, just ignored them and so did Sarah. After the lights were out and Sarah's parents had gone to bed, something strange happened. Sarah liked to collect dolls, preferably rag dolls, and that night Sarah heard voices. 'Sarah, Sarah,' they said. She didn't know whether the voices were real, or if she was imagining it. Obviously not, because suddenly something fell on her. She woke up startled to see a scary-looking figure and without a word she screamed, but no one heard her and the doll started to taunt her. She tried to fight it but she couldn't. She fell to the ground like a ton of bricks.

That morning, when her dad went to wake her up, he wasn't expecting the horrible sight that was about to meet his eyes when he opened his daughter's door. As he opened the door, his whole body felt dead as he saw his beloved Sarah lying dead on the coarse carpet. His heart felt punctured and his face was drained of colour, his blood pressure rocketed and his whole life flashed before his very eyes.

The police had taken a look, but needed to take a further look at the body. They said she died with no injuries.

So just how did she die?

Matthew Jones (11)

Figures

The thumping got louder and louder. I couldn't bear it anymore. They came closer and closer. I woke up in a cold sweat. I thought it had all been a dream, or had it?

My mum was calling me to get out of bed. My room seemed different, it had a funny feeling in it like something had been there. I thought nothing of it. I got ready for school.

As I walked down Walnut Lane, I thought I saw something in the cemetery by my father's grave.

The school was packed as usual. I told my friends about my dream. They said I was just being silly.

When school ended, I walked past the cemetery again. There it was, the figure I had seen earlier.

As I came to my house, I could see police cars. My aunt was there. She said that my mum had been murdered. I ran out of the door and went to the cemetery. The grave where my father had been buried was no longer there; none of the graves were. All of a sudden, a hand grabbed my shoulder. I turned and saw my father and mother. They were pale and looked dead. They took me to a clearing in a wood. There was chanting, it was pounding my ear drums. I was thrown to the floor by the spirits and was bound. I could see a figure coming towards me with what looked like a knife. It all went black …

Hugh Wallis (10)

Am I Dead?

My head hurts and I feel ill and I can't remember anything. All I remember was getting up to go to the toilet, then waking up lying spread out across the landing with something wet and sticky running down my face.

Though, as I swung my legs round to get out of bed, I put my hand down to support myself, I felt something wet. At first I thought I had wet myself, seeing as I had not reached the toilet, except as I turned around to look at it, I saw a crimson-red colour patch. It was almost the same colour as blood! However the patch soon lost my attention because as I turned around, I caught sight of my reflection in the mirror. No, it couldn't be true. I had a black eye, a scar across my forehead and there was blood all over me.

I didn't understand what was going on. I am only 15, yet it looked like someone had tried to assassinate me.

As I went out onto the landing, I saw a kitchen knife hanging out the wall. There was blood splattered everywhere and just at my feet there was another crimson patch. It looked like a war zone, like someone had tried to kill me.

I screamed, but didn't hear anything. Then my brother came out of his room and ran straight through me to my parents' room.

Maybe they tried and succeeded after all.

Felicia Gatenby (12)

The Runaways

The sun was starting to rise, hot blood-reds blending into cheerful warm yellows and cold misty blues, looking like a tie-dyed rug from the hippy generation. All was blanketed in an eerie silence as if the village had a great secret it was not prepared to tell. This remained so until the silence was broken.

'Down here,' panted Karlie.

'Why? We've been running all night, they won't even know we're missing until they wake up,' gasped Roxanne, 'and by then, we'll be long gone.'

The two girls stumbled and tripped along the vast expanse of tarmac, it was beginning to seem like they would never get anywhere, that they would run all their lives but end up where they started. Like a treadmill, the never-ending treadmill that is life.

'Right, help me set up the tent,' Karlie shouted, unpacking a large brown canvas lump from her duffle bag.

The two girls worked together to pitch the tent, but even so, it took them an age, and when they had completed their task, night had fallen and their fingers were numb and cold.

'We need a fire,' both agreed, and for a long time both set about gathering dry wood, stone and fruit, nuts and berries.

Sometime after they began this task, a small flicker of flame began to lick the wood and ignite it. The shadows from the fire created dancing silhouettes on the side of the tent. The moon was full, the air was warm and the aroma of wood smoke drifted. Although there was not a soul around to notice, for from the inside of the tent, snoring could be heard.

Tap, tap, tap. It was Roxanne who heard it first, a constant tapping noise. 'What was that?' she spoke in a whisper.

Then a shadow, a terrifying shadow, shapeless and meaningless, yet it triggered a detailed image in her mind of a leaning figure, arms outstretched, searching for her.

Then the wind, a howling, screeching swoop of surging power, taunting, threatened to lift the flimsy canvas tent and lift it high into the air. *Then drop it?* thought Roxanne.

Down and down and down, faster and faster, hurtling towards the ground! She woke, beads of sweat glistening on her forehead, like the early morning dew caught in a spider's web.

Birds on a nearby tree began to chirrup a sign that night was no more and it was morning. And the start of a new day.

Antonia Dali (11)

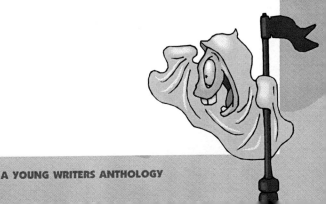

The Last Night Of My Life

Late last night, the night before my 11th birthday, when my mum and dad were asleep and I was reading my book, I heard a snuffle and a crash from the living room. I knew it couldn't have been a dog or a cat because we didn't have any. It might have been one of my presents falling. So I forgot about it.

The noise became louder. Suddenly I heard something creeping up the stairs. It wasn't some presents. I heard a hissing and a bizarre cackling noise. I knew it had feet, but I didn't know anything else.

The crashes and bangs were getting closer and closer. My bedroom door creaked open. I screamed. Nothing happened. The thing was getting closer, shadowing over me. Tall and scaly. I was cornered, I could not move. The creature snatched and grabbed blindly in the dark. I felt its hand hit me and the fingers curling round my waist. I struggled. I could not escape from its tough grasp. The very last thing I ever saw was the monster feasting on my organs.

Jennifer Bullers (10)

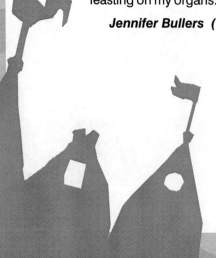

RIP

One night, my family decided to go to my nan's house for the evening. I didn't want to go, so I stayed in the house alone, apart from my obnoxious older brother.

Whilst reading my magazines in bed, I heard a knock on the door. My brother wasn't interested, he was watching his favourite programme in his room. Peering through the window I could see no one. I went back to bed.

Peace didn't last. Hearing the gates of the drive open, I looked out. No one in sight, I started to feel scared.

The phone rang, I answered, no one was on the line. I dropped the phone and shivered.

I looked out of the window. Dark, misty clouds caught my eye, they looked like scary faces. Taking my mind off these silly thoughts, I switched on the television and duly fell asleep.

I woke with a jolt, it was 9am. Where was everyone? I was late for school. I got dressed quickly and scrambled out of the house.

Passing the church, I froze. Family and friends were stood outside, dressed in black and looking very sad. I ran up to them and shouted, 'What are you doing here?' No one listened or took any notice.

A long, elegant black car arrived. Three men carefully lifted out a coffin covered in vivid blue flowers. My favourite colour! But I shrieked when I read the name on the coffin, it read: *Elizabeth Hanrey, RIP.*

Elizabeth Hanrey (10)

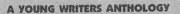

L'Hôtel Hanté

There was a violent storm outside. Mr and Mrs Nett entered a small hotel near an oak tree. Inside, everything was antique. They were greeted by a lady with a bun.

'My name is Marie Fantôme and this is my daughter Annette, who shall take you to a room,' she said.

Annette had dark hair which contrasted her pale face. She led them up the creaky staircase by candlelight. 'How long are you staying?' she asked.

'Just the night,' said Mr Nett. 'We are going to visit the Eiffel Tower tomorrow, and then go home.'

'Eiffel Tower?' said Annette. 'I have never heard of it.'

How odd. They reached a room with a feather bed and two candles. *There must be a power outage,* thought Mrs Nett. The couple fell asleep through the storm.

The next morning, they awoke and got their luggage downstairs.

'500 Francs please,' smiled Madame Fantôme.

'Oh, we thought you'd converted to Euros,' said Mr Nett in a confused tone.

However, Marie accepted the Euros uncertainly.

Mr and Mrs Nett drove to Paris and were on their way to the Euro Tunnel when Mrs Nett decided to drop off a postcard of the Eiffel Tower for Annette. They drove up to the hotel, when Mr Nett gave a gasp. The hotel had disappeared! All that stood was the oak tree and a historic plaque which read: *Site of L'Hôtel Hanté, Property of Marie Fantôme 1750-1790 and her daughter Annette Fantôme 1773-1790, died due to the plague of 1790.*

Rachna Y Joshi (15)

Fated-Doom

Through the murky passageway it stood, and it stood silently …

What was it? Perhaps a banshee, a ghost, or maybe just maybe, another ingenious creation of her mentality. The possibilities were endless, her heart was now pounding, and with every beat of her eyes were tightening with crimson blood. The whispers of the wind were like a thousand untamed brutes slowing rising to meet her doom.

It moved …

Her eyes pounced as she tried to pursue the gloomy shadows, shadows that belonged in only one place - *Hell!*

The silence was torturing her. Why her? Why today? Why here?

A razor-sharp image appeared in front of her in the darkness, it murmured as if it was in pain. The creature entered the light.

'You?' her voice echoed sharply through the blunt air.

Kanda Ahmed (14)

Buried Alive

Liza and Shaz broke into a dead run. Breaking the tense silence that surrounded them, their breaths came in little short gasps. Shaz stopped and searched her surroundings and turned to Liza. 'Dead end,' she announced. 'Liza?' she called, raising her voice slightly. 'Liza?' she called again. But there was no sign of her. She was … gone. Just like that, she had disappeared.

Shaz started to panic, desperately searching for her. *Where is she?* Shaz thought. *Does he have her? No,* she thought, *I can't think like this. I must be strong.* But even as she thought those words she was shaking, shaking at the idea of her being caught. Caught by what they had worked so hard to escape from. She could feel the fear welling up inside her as she heard leaves crunch under heavy footsteps. Tears trickled down her face as she saw a figure emerge from the shadows of the trees. Her heart threatened to burst through her chest as she realised that grotesque figure was *her*, Liza. But before she could convey her confusion in words, she fell unconscious from a hard blow to her head …

Once she woke up, she was lying down; on something soft. But trapped. Suffocating. In the company of the darkness. Her imagination took hold of her as sinister ideas popped up in her mind, but nothing could have prepared her for what she heard next.

'… Earth to earth, ashes to ashes, dust to dust …'

Chorin Kawa (14)

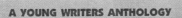

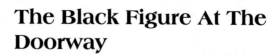

The Black Figure At The Doorway

Coming home from a concert, singing along with my mum to the radio, the radio cut off. Suddenly, the car started to judder to a halt. We had run out of petrol. It was dark and we'd just passed a petrol station about two miles away. Mum got the petrol can and told me to stay in the car.

Ninety minutes later, Mum still hadn't come back, so I set out to find her. There was a flicker of light upon a hill, so I decided to investigate.

As it turned midnight, owls started to hoot. *Boom, boom, bang!* A storm just started. I was so scared I wet myself.

As I was gradually coming to a forest, my hair stood straight on the back of my neck and my nerves were up to a maximum. I ran through, it never stopped going on and on until a barn appeared. *Boom, boom* on the iron door. Nobody was there. I decided to walk into the barn which was full of cobwebs and spiders, to get shelter, it was worth it.

Turning round to find somewhere to sit, I got tangled up. Seeing a figure at the door, I screamed. Pinning up against the wall, the figure grew bigger. Suddenly there was a croaky voice (like a witch's) saying, 'Jade, is that you?'

Now, seeing just a head, I grew still.

With a cough, followed by, 'Jade, it's your mum!' relief swam through me. I'll never disobey my mum again.

Jade Mullen (11)

Lady In Black

Once upon a time there was a girl called Mary. She believed in all kinds of things, such as ghosts.

One stormy night there was a tap on the window. Mary climbed out of her creaky old bed and peered out of the curtain. She could just make out a shadowy figure. Mary had a closer look, it had gone. Mary climbed into bed and fell into a deep sleep. In her sleep she had a dream, she pictured the shadowy picture she saw from her window, it came closer and closer. At this point, Mary was tossing and turning in her bed. The figure was following her. In her dream something strange happened. Mary dreamt she was walking through a graveyard, now she could see the figure, it was a woman in a long black cloak. Mary started running, the figure ran after her. Mary started screaming, the figure drew closer, it moved like lightning. Suddenly, a ghost came up behind her, this one was white. It tried slowing the other figure down. It almost seemed it was trying to protect Mary, in a scary kind of way.

Mary woke up, but did not notice she was in the white ghost's long, baggy, white arms.

Jade Huckin (10)

The Mansion Of No Returns

On a cold, gloomy Sunday morning in a dark forest where a tall mansion stood, two 12-year-old girls came skipping happily along. As the two girls reached the mansion, they stopped in their tracks, they felt a cold chill rush through them. The mansion they were standing in front of was the Mansion of No Returns. People went in, but never came out, but these girls would never give up.

The two girls slowly walked up the stairs, as they opened the door lots of bats flew out. As they walked into the mansion, the door slammed behind them with a big bang. They walked into the maid's room, an old man was lying dead on the floor. The two girls screamed as they saw a ghost appear out of nowhere. The room was spinning around and around, they were running as fast as they could, trying to find an exit, pulling on a door as quickly as they could.

The door flung open, they ran out of the mansion and back into the forest, the ghost was still chasing them. The ghost suddenly flew in the opposite direction as an old man came strolling by with his dog. The girls ran over to the old man and told him what had happened.

The old man replied, 'There's nothing behind you, you crazy kids!' and walked off in a strop with his dog.

The girls walked off slowly, still with the image in their heads.

Paige-Louise Fox (12)

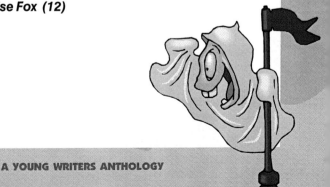

School Plan

'Stop it Sara!' said Mrs Thomas. 'I've told you time after time not to shout out.'

Sara thought Mrs Thomas was not a very nice teacher as she was always telling her off. Sara said to herself it was time to stop letting Mrs Thomas tell her off, she was going to make a plan with her friend Laura.

As Laura and Sara went upstairs to make their plan, the teachers back in the school were talking about how badly behaved Sara had been during school today.

The next day, after school, they went back home for tea, so their parents weren't suspicious.

At school, it was 7pm and getting dark. They had put glue on Mrs Thomas' chair and had decided on some tricks. They were just about to leave as they heard a scream from around the corner.

They ran, but the closer they ran to the door, the louder the screaming became. They saw a ghost, all fuzzy and grey. It went through Laura and she fell to the floor in a heap. As Sara picked Laura up, they realised that the only exit left was in Mrs Thomas' room above the chair with the glue on. With great difficulty, they climbed through the small exit. The ghosts were screaming and windows were breaking.

Finally they got out and by this time, police were surrounding the school. When they got home they were in real trouble, and the next day, were in worse trouble at school.

Emily Tune (13)

A Ghost Story

I didn't like going on holiday. This time it was a mansion up in the mountains. On the final day, I switched off the light to go to bed.

Suddenly I shot up and looked out of the window. The lonely streets were dark and wet, and the street lamps lit up the footpaths. I turned around, the clock said 3am.

I crawled back into bed, when I saw a glowing sign … I zoomed out of bed and switched on the light and saw a message that said, 'Be warned'. Suddenly, a man appeared.

'Aarrgghhh!' I screeched. The lights switched off and back on, there was nothing there.

The next morning I went shopping with my new friend I'd met on holiday and forgot all about it.

There was a new shop in town. As we walked past it, I saw the same sign and the same man as from the night before. Without warning, the shop exploded. The man went up with it!

Michael Saunders (10)

A Ghost Story

It was dark, quite late. Rachel lived in Manchester, in her old house. She got into the bath. Her mother and father had gone away for two weeks.

The time on the clock in the bathroom was 11.30 and all of a sudden she saw a shadow running across the room. At first she thought it was nothing, until the shadow appeared again.

Bang. The lights went off, and then all the electricity went off. She held her breath and the lights came back on.

'What is that running across the room?' Rachel whispered to herself. 'What's going on? What do you want?'

Rachel looked for the shadow and when she found it she shouted, 'Oi you, leave me alone, go away from me you horrible thing.'

'No!' it replied.

At 3.30pm the next day she went shopping at the supermarket for some food, and she wanted to treat herself so she bought some shoes. Then she went to get the food. She had finished all of her shopping.

Suddenly, she saw exactly the same shadow. She pressed the button for the lift and at her pick-up point, when the lift doors opened, the shadow was there.

The shadow said, 'You can only just about fit in here.'

Rachel replied, 'No thanks, I'll walk down.'

The lift went down and crashed, and the people that were in it died.

Rachel went home. She was in the bath, she saw a shadow running across the room …

Rebecca Broome (9)

A Ghost Story

It was midnight. I was in a mansion above town. I was in bed, reading, I couldn't sleep. As the grandfather clock struck 12, I heard a rumble of thunder and saw a flash of lightning, and my room lit up. I heard loads of bangs, so I went to the window. It was hailstones. I saw my 4x4 soaking wet.

Just as I got back into bed, there was a loud bang! I ran to the window. A hearse had crashed into the wall. I opened the window and hid behind the shutters. The driver had no face. He saw me and shouted, 'Can I use your 4x4?'

'No!' I shouted, and jumped back into bed.

The next morning, I thought it was all a dream. I had my breakfast and went shopping in town. I went to the seventh floor to buy clothes and trainers. Once I'd finished, I had six bags full. I had three in each hand. I went to the elevator to go down to the bottom floor to exit the building. The doors opened, it was full of people. The lift assistant had no face. It was the hearse driver! I recognised him and said, 'I'll go down the stairs, all right?'

The doors closed. The fire alarm went off, then *bang!* The electrics blew up and the right side of the building collapsed. Everyone was killed but the hearse driver.

Ben Pearce (10)

The Flesh-Eating Screamer

I set up camp in the middle of the woods. It was awfully cold, dark, and very misty. I got to sleep in the end but suddenly, *tap, tap, tap,* on the side of the tent. It woke me up. I thought it was my dog, but then I saw that there was nothing left of him, but his one leg bone.

Something suddenly screamed and very quickly, a glowing, wavy shadow shot towards my tent. There was another *tap, tap, tap*, and it went back again and did this several times. The last time he came towards the door of the tent and reached for the zip. I got closer to the door. I saw the creature had ten eyes. It started to open the door. I fought to pull the zip back down, but it was an alien life form, it was too strong and broke the zip from the inside.

Luckily, very luckily, I had two pieces of chicken and a sunroof in the top of the tent. I threw them both out and it chased after them. I got out and ran as fast as I could. I was thinking to myself, *I've lost him.* All of a sudden, *bang!* I ran straight into him. He grabbed me and put a rope around my legs and hands, then put a bag over my head, it wouldn't break. He took me to his ship and took all the rope and bag off me. I ran home and I never saw the creature again.

Harley King (10)

The Haunted Hotel

It all started in Florida. It was our first week. We were in a hotel in a town called Boca Raton. There were rumours going around that the hotel was haunted. We had always wanted to see a ghost or a spirit, so we decided to set up the video camera and get it on film.

The next night we couldn't sleep, so we decided to talk about all the rumours, when suddenly we heard footsteps coming up the stairs.

We thought it was other people coming up the stairs. We looked out the door and saw this little girl walking towards our room. We knew it was a ghost because we could see straight through her. We were so scared we went and hid in the closet. We knew we had always wanted to get a ghost on film. Since I was the smallest, I had to try and sneak past her and get the camera, but that didn't work out as planned. The girl saw me and followed me to my parents' room. I grabbed the camera and videoed her for about two minutes then I passed out.

I woke up the next morning wondering what had happened. I got dressed and went to the café. We enjoyed our holiday.

We went home and I told all of my friends. They didn't believe me at first, until I showed them the tape, and from this day on I still wonder, was it a dream, or a real ghost?

Shannon Murphy (10)

Can You See Me Now?

Max Edwards was paranoid. As much as he wanted to enjoy his body before old age imprisoned it, he felt there wasn't much to celebrate about his pallid, gangly features and foul-smelling, oily skin. And so, he murdered anyone who looked upon him in such a way that would make him feel uneasy or out of place.

It was strange how a simple schoolboy could achieve such ghastly stealth missions without ever getting caught. Most teenagers resorted to truanting, so they could hide somewhere and cry. But Max wasn't most teenagers. Instead, he would slip on a balaclava, follow his victim till they were alone, then bring down a sharp blow to the innocent's head, using whatever was handy at the time. This didn't kill them though. *Oh no.* Max relished dragging his victim into the nearby woods, where he'd use a knife to gouge out their frightened eyes.

'That'll teach you for staring at me,' he'd maliciously whisper in their ear. Then, just before performing the last part of the ritual, he'd hiss, *'Can you see me now?'*

The muffled screaming from their bound mouth was always his signal. He'd flash his knife in the moonlight and aggressively end his victim's life.

Finishing the job off by insultingly placing a few handfuls of crispy brown leaves over the corpse, he'd speak to the surrounding area, 'Don't judge people before you know them.'

But no one was listening. And no one ever will.

Karla Brading (16)

The Curse Of The Black Ghost

The dustbins rattled like something was trying to get out from behind them. My heart started thumping, I was being watched. I started to panic and ran as fast as I could. I peered over my shoulder. A massive, black, slimy arm was reaching towards me. I could not run anymore, my legs were shaking like pins. I could not keep my balance and stumbled headfirst in a pile of rubbish.

Two weeks later …

'Where am I?' I muttered, slowly getting up. I was in hospital. A tall, grim, old nurse marched towards me, she reminded me of my school teacher.

'Mrs Price,' called a tall African man. 'Hello, my name is Dr Richards. I am new, is this my patient?'

She nodded and without a word, marched off again.

Dr Richards' kind face turned as pale as a ghost's. I shrieked in horror, I was so terrified I couldn't move. He grinned and grinned, his frightful smile growing wider and wider. Suddenly, those awful black arms popped out of his sides. He grasped me tight and then strangely softened his grip, and a deep, frightened voice asked for help.

'Help me, I am cursed. I may never rest in peace unless you destroy this medallion. Please save me, or I will pass the curse down to you.'

That night, I shared the secret with my sister Anna. We both roughly look the same, long brown hair and a peachy-coloured skin.

'Emily, let's go down to the garage and we could use some tools to destroy the medallion,' Anna said, putting her coat on.

I agreed, and we both quietly made our way down.

Anna grabbed a hammer and swung it high, by mistake it knocked a tin of red paint off the shelf, it covered us both. I grabbed the hammer from her and with a loud smash, the medallion broke.

With a huge shock I leaped out of my bed and muttered softly to myself, 'It was just a dream.' In astonishment, I noticed I was covered in bright red paint!

Charlotte Appleyard (11)

The Onlookers

It was coming towards me. Eyes burning yellow through the pouring rain, glaring at me, staring through the darkness right at me. Its hulking mass hurtled ever nearer. What could I do? I could smell its terrible breath, thick and grey, clouding out behind it. Its rumbling growl making the ground tremble, making *me* tremble. And still it came, chewing up the road, closer and closer. I could feel the sticky heat of the thing as it bore down upon me, but I couldn't run, I could only curl up into a tiny ball and wait for it. Eyes tightly shut, head tucked down. *Splat!* My eye rolled into the middle of the road. My leg flew into the hedge; the rest of me was smeared along the road like strawberry jam on toast.

And that was the end of me, Harry Hedgehog the 523rd gone forever, no more. That was last Hallowe'en, and now I haunt this road. For years my ancestors have been trying to cross here. Right now, I am watching Harry the 524th follow in my footsteps to his gory end. If only he'd stayed at home, if only *I'd* stayed at home …

Now I have another onlooker.

Miri Wakelin-Gilden (10)

Blue Moon

One gloomy night on a dark hill far away lay the black shadow of a castle. Every full moon the castle would appear and creepy noises would be heard from inside it. On that night it happened to be the night of a blue moon. The castle appeared like it did every full moon, but tonight was no ordinary night.

There was a squeal of brakes at the great black gates as a man parked his car. He got out of his car and pulled at the gates. They opened with a creak and he walked in. He trudged up the path of the crumbling gravel to the big oak door. As soon as he touched the gold knocker, the door opened. Slowly he walked in. It was pitch-black apart from one flickering candle in the distance. Suddenly there was the sound of slamming doors and dripping water. The man was so scared that he turned to run, but as he turned, there in front of him was a ghostly white figure. It looked like a butler. The man screamed, dodged the figure and ran for the door. He ran down the path of crumbling gravel and hauled open the gates. He got into his car and there was a horrible cackle. He drove off as fast as he could. There was a sudden flash of lightning and then everything vanished, the castle, the path with the crumbling gravel and the huge black gates, but the shadow still remains there today.

Jessica Ball (11)

Scary Book

It all happened on Hallowe'en. Bob, Stacey, James and Laura were all driving in a car, then *boom!* They hit something. They jumped out. There was a man lying on the floor. He was *just* alive.

He said, 'I'm going to get you …' Then he died.

The four teenagers picked up the body and buried him.

When they were driving home, James needed a tinkle so out he got and went. Five minutes later the others heard a shout, then it started to rain. There was a rustle in the bush. All of a sudden a body was thrown at the car. It broke the windscreen, but the body looked like James!

Bob drove on as fast as possible, then Laura fell out of the car. Then the ghost of the guy they'd killed came out of nowhere but with a knife.

Laura ran but she stopped and shouted out, 'Hold on, my shoelace has come undone.' She bent over and tied a knot and carried on running.

Moments later Stacey looked back and Laura was on the floor, dead. Bob pushed the pedal to the metal. It all went as cold as an ice cream in a freezer and the car door where Stacey was sitting opened and she fell out.

The ice cream feeling happened again and Bob just made it into the town and the feeling went away. Bob was safe and alive.

The ghost still haunts him even now.

Elliot Stockford (11)

Scaredy-Cat

Once upon a time there was a girl named Vicky. She had a best friend called Emma. Next to Vicky's house was a graveyard. Emma was round Vicky's house that afternoon. About 7pm they decided to walk down to the shops. On the way they passed the graveyard.

'Come on, let's have a look around,' Vicky said to Emma.

'No, let's just go down to the shops,' Emma said.

'Scaredy-cat! Scaredy-cat!'

'Fine, if I have to, but only for a few minutes.'

They both went into the graveyard. Vicky was laughing and jumping around the gravestones. Emma was terrified.

There was a little stone building at the end of the cemetery. Vicky dared Emma to go in.

'No,' Emma said.

Vicky started to shout scaredy-cat again.

Emma shouted in a scared voice, 'Fine, I will go in.'

As she was walking between the gravestones her back was shivering, she was as pale as a ghost. She walked in. Suddenly there was a big bang and Emma disappeared. Vicky yelled for help, but no one came. She didn't know what to do so she ran all the way home.

The next night something came to visit her. It wasn't the tooth fairy - it was Emma as a ghost! She had come to haunt Vicky for daring her to go in the little stone building.

Chloe Isgrove (12)

The Haunted Manor

It was midnight. Alex and his friends, Jack, Ben, Sam and Dan were sharing a room in a manor house. They had been invited there for three nights. Alex was awake, he could not sleep. He left the room to go to the toilet and heard faint laughter from the lounge. No one was up though and Alex knew that.

Suddenly all the lights dimmed. This was not normal. The laughter turned into a scream. Alex froze. He ran back into his room.

Jack was awake. 'What's going on?' he groaned.

'Did you not hear the screams Jack?'

'What screams? No one's screamed, just go to bed, all right.'

Alex turned round and opened the door. A movement. To Alex's horror he saw a completely pale figure standing in front of him. It stumbled forward and gently touched his shoulder. A stone-cold chill ran down Alex's spine. He felt sick. Alex seemed to be fading. The figure disappeared.

It seemed Alex had been infected with the same thing. He screamed. That was the last thing he did before he was gone.

Still spine-chilling screams run through the manor every midnight and one more gets infected never to be seen again.

Gregory Winter (11)

I Tooth

I went to Sam's house last night, it was big, like a castle.

Sam said, 'Let's go up to the top tower.'

'No!' I refused. 'You know what happens when you go up there!' I refused again.

'Last night I saw I Tooth. I Tooth was there, staring at me.'

I didn't want to go but Sam dragged me with him.

When we got to the second set of stairs, he started shaking, shaking with fear.

I said, 'You wanted to go up so we will go up together.' I dragged him up. When we were nearly at the top, I said, 'It is your turn to drag me now.'

When we were at the top I screamed.

Sam's mother heard the screams and she came running. All she found were two dead bodies.

Do you want to know how I am writing this story? Well, maybe it's because I'm a ghost!

Alice Brock (9)

Ghost Chase Revealed

It was 11pm. I went upstairs to my bedroom, closed the curtains and got into bed. I saw a shadow, so I got out of bed and had a look. There was nothing there. I scurried back into bed. It was there again. I took no notice of it.

I heard a cry from downstairs and a screech that came from the bathroom. I quickly went to see what it was, because my mum was in the bathroom, but she was gone. I was really scared. I went back in my room.

Carefully a mysterious man came into my room. I quickly sprinted out to my mum's room. He followed. He held my mum's hand. Then mine. I turned to my mum, but she was gone. I cried. I searched and searched, no sign of the man, no sign of my mum.

I went back in my mum's room again, then I fell asleep. I woke about 1am. I heard another screech. The man appeared and pulled me out of bed. I think he was saving me from something. I screamed.

He whispered, 'Don't worry, you'll be safe.'

'Where's my mum?' I whispered.

'You'll find out,' he said.

I was afraid. We went to the basement. There was a bang, clang and then a thud, then silence and it went pitch-black. Then I heard another crash. I couldn't move, I was stuck. We all got rushed to the hospital.

The next morning we were allowed out. We lived in horror once again.

Ellie Davis (9)

The Haunted House

Daniel, Karen and Tracey had decided to go on a camping trip into the woods at the weekend. As they were driving in their camper van, they suddenly broke down in the middle of nowhere.

'What shall we do now?' said Karen to Daniel in a panicky voice.

'Don't panic,' Daniel said calmly. 'We'll find a house and ask to use their phone.'

As they started walking, Tracey stumbled over a broken branch. 'I think I've sprained my ankle,' she cried.

'We'll have to sit down for a while,' said Daniel.

'Looks like a storm is coming,' said Karen.

Daniel helped Tracey up and led them through the forest. As the storm started to rage, Tracey spotted an old mansion out of the corner of her eye. It was next to a graveyard.

'It looks like it's been there for hundreds of years,' exclaimed Daniel.

'I bet your grandma used to live there,' joked Karen.

Daniel smirked and carried on walking to the mansion.

As they got to the big, brown, dusty, old door, their hearts started to pound.

'This looks really creepy,' said Tracey in a shaky voice.

They knocked on a big rusty knocker, the door creaked open slightly.

Karen jumped, 'I don't think this is a good idea,' she said quietly as Daniel encouraged them to go in.

They saw a big staircase covered in cobwebs.

'Looks like the cleaning ladies' century off,' joked Daniel, trying to make the others feel at ease.

As they went up the staircase, Tracey screamed because with every step she took there would be a creak. Daniel made Tracey sit down to take a breath and told her to calm down.

They went into a room, it was small, dark and had a musty smell.

'Atishoo!' sneezed Karen. 'It's very dusty in here.'

'Look, there's an old lantern,' said Daniel.

Tracey spotted a big old wardrobe. 'I feel like someone's watching over me,' she cried.

Daniel walked over to the wardrobe and was about to open the doors to show Tracey there was nothing to be afraid of as the wardrobe creaked open slowly. Out fell a skeleton. Both girls screamed with fear and clung to each other behind Daniel. As the skeleton fell on Daniel, a piercing screech filled the room. The girls screamed in sheer terror.

'Oh my gosh, what was that noise? Where did it come from?' shouted Karen. '*Let's get out of here,* before anything else happens.'

Daniel, Tracey and Karen ran out of the mansion as fast as they could and ran so far until the mansion was out of sight. As they were running, what they didn't notice was an old woman watching them run from the upstairs window of the old mansion. It was the ghost of the lady who'd lived there and died in that same wardrobe in 1894.

Bernadette Sayers (10)

Uncle Keith

Everyone said the house was haunted, but I found it hard to believe them. I decided to find out for myself. First I had to decide when to go. I looked up at the calendar. This Saturday, Dad said the whole day was up to me. I was sure Dad wouldn't be surprised if I wasn't in the house all day. Just in case, I'd leave a note saying that I'd be having a sleepover at my friend's.

It was Wednesday. There were only three more days to go till Saturday. Boy, I was excited. Friday night, I set my alarm at six. I slithered into bed waiting for the next day. I woke with a shock. I could see the early morning dew trickling down my misted window. A burst of excitement raced through me. I got up briskly, had a shower, brushed my teeth and had a large bowl of cornflakes. I loaded my rucksack with food, torch, a camera and my mobile phone. Time was ticking by, it was half-past six. I pulled on my jacket and shoes and set off.

As I crept along the silent streets, I had a feeling of warning brush my brain, but that didn't really bother me. When I arrived at the house of mystery, it seemed very spooky, even in broad daylight. I walked up the grey and miserable stone steps. For a split second I thought I had lost my bravery. I was urging myself to run down the steps. My legs were out of control. They were carrying me towards the huge iron doors. I closed my eyes. I heard the sound of an ancient door squeaking open. My eyelids forced open. Cobwebs were cloaking over most of the old furniture. A flood of panic showered me. *Bang!* The door had closed shut.

'Aha! Just as I expected, Roxanne!' shot a voice at me.

'Argh!'

'Hush girl! Don't spoil the silence,' hissed the ghost.

'W-who are you?' I sputtered.

'A ghost, can't you see?' it smirked.

'Yes, but you look very -'

'Very what?' he snapped.

'Very familiar,' I said.

'Oh, clever one, well spotted. I think it's time I introduced myself, my name is Keith,' he said as he shot a smug look at me.

'Wait a minute, I know that Dad was talking to me about someone called Keith,' I said.

'Yes, I am your great, great uncle, Roxanne.' He smiled.

'Uncle Keith,' she breathed. 'You were the one to master judo, kung fu and karate.'

'Yes, yes all that fun I used to have. Marvellous!'

I felt quite tired after having the world's most boring tea with her great uncle. It only lasted fifteen minutes. I stretched as she reached for her watch. *What? Seven-thirty already?* I screamed.

'You never feel time go by here,' said Keith.

'I've got to go,' I said with panic. 'Nice meeting you, Uncle Keith.'

'You can only leave if you promise to visit me regularly, Roxanne,' said the spooky ghost.

'Fine. Deal. Every Saturday. Not always, because I might be ill. OK?'

'You are free to leave, Roxanne,' said Keith.

'I'll see you next week!'

Venezia Souceradjou (12)

A Ghost Story

One dark, gloomy night the wind is howling and there are no houses for miles and miles. You wish you had never moved into the cold, echoing mansion. Faint cackles can be heard echoing around the mansion. You try to get to sleep that night but it is impossible.

The next day you take your dog called Robbie, a Westie, for a walk. At the top of the hill there is a bench. You sit down on it, looking at the countryside with Robbie lying next to you. Suddenly, without warning, Robbie runs back to the mansion. You chase after Robbie.

You finally get back to the mansion. You see blood over all the walls. You decide to hunt round the house for Robbie. Robbie starts whimpering. Someone or at least some thing is talking. Your dog is gone. Robbie is nowhere to be seen. White faces are watching you.

Is this the end or is it only the beginning?

Andrew Puk (9)

A Ghost Story

'Michael! Michael! Are you playing or what?'

'Sorry Pete, I was daydreaming.'

'Again, Michael?'

'Yeah, sorry about that. Hey! Where's dinner?' I asked.

'Trust you to be thinking of your stomach. Anyway you've got to go home now.'

I grumbled (or maybe my stomach did), put on my coat and slammed the door and started on the five minute walk to the bus stop.

It was already black and the leaves rattled noisily in the trees all around me. When I got to the bus stop I sat heavily down and waited. I began to get tired and lay down on the bench. Just as I closed my eyes I saw the lights of the bus and I heard the screeching of the brakes. According to my watch it was 3 hours later, but too tired to care I hopped on and turned to the driver, but there wasn't one. I looked properly and I was in 'Dead or Alive 3', a video game I'd played lots of times.

A big voice boomed out, 'Get across to the other side and you win a giant beefburger.'

A big spotlight pointed it out. I had 2 minutes to duck under slashing swords, jump on stepping stones with crocodiles trying to gobble me up and much more. I ducked, I dived, I jumped and touched it! No … !

Athena Draper (9)

Killerman

As the small rusty door handle rotated from one angle to another, the door slowly opened. A colossal hairy hand crept out from behind the doorway. Now an arm, huge, as big as an elephant's trunk. The body started to emerge from the darkness, but no, it couldn't be, yes, it was the monster from the dark and mysterious hole in the floorboards - Killerman! Running frantically I leapt into the hole without stopping to look back.

It was dark and gloomy down in the hole, penetrating coldness touched my dry lips. Killerman howled into the moonlight and came charging towards the hole. I could not see so I quickly felt for a wall. Then I found what I was looking for, a door handle. I turned the gleaming handle and it opened into the bright light. It was so bright I could see worse than I could in the darkness. I stepped forwards. Then I felt it, the sharp narrow tooth of, of, of, Killerman …

Jacob Norris (9)

Spooky Dream

One Hallowe'en night, me, my mum, dad, brother and sister went to this spooky hotel. We went trick or treating and went back to the hotel. By the time we got back it was midnight so we got in bed and we went to sleep, but I didn't because I heard howling noises. It turned out to be just the wind. I heard a creaking noise, but it was the door. I saw a flying figure and guess what? It was *a bat!* A hairy, giant bat was flying around the room.

My mum got up and said, 'That's it. We are going home.'

We got up and opened the closet door and what popped out? A skeleton! My brother and I laughed but my mum was furious.

We tried to ring for a taxi but the telephone line was cut so we had to walk to the airport but it wasn't very far. about twenty minutes in the cold, wet rain.

As we walked, the lights started to flicker. It was very scary. We could hear footsteps behind us so we ran as the footsteps came closer. We saw the airport and this old man with a gun. I woke up. Was it all a dream? Did it really happen? I didn't know, maybe I'd eaten too much candy and had a nightmare. I got up and went to the kitchen and what was there on the table? *The old man!*

Shannon Rocks (10)

What Was That?

In an old rectory there was a graveyard as the back garden. The haunted rectory was big. Everybody was scared stiff of it. The two best friends tiptoed into the graveyard.

The beech trees were hovering over every grave that was laid. When the wind blew and the night was stormy the best friends were still up and were frightened. They sat in the lounge with the fire on, then the picture above the mantelpiece fell off, all of a sudden they heard a scream.

They both ran upstairs but no one was there and there wasn't any proof anyone had been there; so they went downstairs again and started talking about what had just happened.

'That was weird!' said Amy.

'Yeah, I know,' replied Chloe.

'Argh!' Amy screamed at the top of her voice.

'The eyes on that picture just moved!' yelped Chloe.

They both ran into the kitchen and locked the door. In the corner of the kitchen was a ghost with a knife. It started coming towards them slowly. They tried to unlock the door but it was too stiff so they screamed in a high voice and the ghost disappeared. Also the door swung open and Amy and Chloe ran home!

Charlotte Sansom (11)

The House Next Door

It was a bright spring day, the sound of children and birdsong filled the air. The family was very excited because a family was moving in next door. A delivery van came. The family, Lucy and Paul (children), Steve and Margaret (adults), were so excited to meet them.

They went and knocked on the door. There was no reply. They tried the next day but still no reply. Paul was very suspicious, Lucy and Paul decided to try again later. They approached the house which looked much darker and gloomier than before. The door opened as Paul approached, he backed off but Lucy walked in without looking back.

'Lucy! Stop, wait for me,' Paul cried.

Lucy walked on, but then came to a halt. Paul noticed a glint of red in Lucy's eyes as she looked at a mysterious figure at the back of the hall that she had led Paul into.

'Lucy, what's happening? What are you doing?' Paul cried.

Lucy walked towards the figure and Paul ran after her. As they got nearer they saw the figure was a statue of a man with a sinister grin. An eerie moaning noise filled the hall. It was from behind them, a man limped towards him and Paul thought it was his neighbour but he was dismembered and smelt of rotten flesh. He was coming towards him and he had nowhere to hide …

Remed Ali (11)

The Haunted Mansion

One stormy night a ghost appeared at Draton Manor.

Back at Rachel's house, Rachel and her best friends, Maddie and Zoe were watching telly when there was an urgent newsflash about the haunted manor a few blocks down from where Rachel lived.

We have interrupted your programme to bring you this newsflash,' cried the reporter. 'Draton Manor has once again been the place of a child's abduction. Last night a young boy was snatched on Ty Draw Road and taken to the manor to be tortured. If I was you I would …' The TV reporter froze as a ghost came onto the telly.

'Rachel, that's your road!' Zoe shook.

'Yeah, but don't worry, I've lived here my whole life and I'm still here.'

A creaking noise could be heard from the attic. Maddie screamed! A ghost came down the stairs and grabbed Rachel and Maddie but left Zoe behind. Dun, dun, dun!

The ghost carried the girls away to the manor.

'Leave us alone!' screamed Rachel.

'Don't tell me what to do!' bellowed the ghost.

He threw them into the dungeon to starve, but Zoe, who had been hiding, was on her way. She rescued the girls out of the trapdoor, but the ghost saw. He pulled them to the floor. Next thing they knew they were back in their rooms but they don't know what happened.

Still the ghost roams, even now.

Rachel Gleeson (11)

The Haunted House

On one dark, cold, wintry night, the full moon was shining through Zoe Leverett's attic window. Her two best friends, Rachel and Maddie were sleeping over at her house. They were having a delicious midnight feast with lollies and sweets and crisps until suddenly, Maddie heard something coming from the attic above them. They all stopped chomping, it was silent, there was a creak in the floorboards above.

Zoe told her two shaking friends, 'Let's go into the attic and see what's going on, it's probably nothing.'

Maddie and Rachel looked at each other and answered, 'OK.'

Rachel grabbed a torch. They slowly opened the door and stepped out of the bedroom. They stayed together as they slowly walked up the stairs to the attic. The creaking got louder and louder. Zoe slowly opened the old door. Suddenly the torch went out, it was flung across the room. Out of thin air a ghost appeared! The girls screamed. Zoe ran as fast as she could, she grabbed the torch, she threw it to Rachel, Rachel turned and pressed a button on the wall. A bright light switched on. The ghost screamed and vanished into thin air. The girls ran together to the door. They turned off the light and slowly walked down the stairs. They were still shaking in shock, but after a while they fell asleep.

They will never forget that night and will stay best friends forever.

Zoe Leverett (11)

The Note

It was a dark night, clouds shrouded the moon like a cape, a fork of lightning could be seen on the moors.

The door creaked slightly in the wind and suddenly it shut, as though an invisible hand had pushed it. All three children gasped slightly, shaking as the room became ever so much colder.

'I don't like this,' whispered one as the rocking chair swayed back and forth.

Without warning, the floorboards creaked and a faint mist descended on the children. The match the boy was holding mysteriously blew out.

Then, from the mist, came a figure hovering an inch or two from the floorboards. Its clothes were dated and tatty, the shoes scuffed and worn. As the children stared in horror, their gaze unluckily fell upon its face ... the mouth and jawbone were twisted in a scream. Its eyes sunk deep into its skull.

But, as quickly as it had come, it disappeared. Though the ghost had gone, a piece of parchment fluttered to the ground. One child tiptoed over to it and picked it up. It read 'Meet me at Castell Coch, midnight'. The same note that the three children had found in a tree on the moors.

An icy wind suddenly blew through the room and a figure stood at the door. A scream was the last that was heard of the children.

To this day, if you listen on a moonless, stormy night you can sometimes hear the screams of the children coming from the tower.

Michael Coliandris (11)

The Diamond Ring

The wind was howling like a werewolf in the night when Matt and Jacob were walking their dog Harvey. He was a golden Labrador. He was a big muscular dog and his shoulders were broad. As Harvey tugged on the lead Matt was pulling him back. Jacob was looking round at the atmosphere. He was 11, Matt, Jacob's older brother, was 14. He was stockily built.

They were coming up to the part Jacob hated, *the cemetery.* It was 9pm by now and it had started to get cold. As they walked past the cemetery they noticed something shining near one of the gravestones. It was a 50 carat gold ring with a very expensive diamond in it. They climbed over the big black gates. The small breeze suddenly became a thundering storm.

Then drastically, horrifying zombies and ghosts exited their graves and were calling, 'Freedom!' There was one ghost leading them. He towered over his army and looked Matt and Jacob straight in the eye. Matt and Jacob ran for their lives, but their lives had ended. Zombies sucked the life out of Matt's body. They were left with a heap of skin. Ghosts dropped a gravestone on Jacob's body. Blood spurted out everywhere. The zombies were dripping with blood, as this event didn't happen very often.

Harvey's short fur left him whimpering in the darkness as he ran home. The ring wasn't found, but *you* could find it.

James Humphry (12)

The Subaru Impreza

In a large house on the outskirts of Bristol lived a boy called Marcus Jones. His life revolved around Subaru Imprezas. He had several models and so many photos they were like wallpaper.

On his 21st birthday he received £20,000. He didn't have to think about what to buy - a blue Subaru Impreza with gold wheels.

A dream changed it all though. In it he was driving his blue Impreza with gold wheels. The number plate was MJ21. Suddenly a ghost appeared in the passenger seat saying, 'I mean no harm. I am warning you of danger in your future. Do not buy the Subaru.'

'Why …?'

The ghost disappeared. Marcus turned back to the road. A sudden sharp turn was imminent. He pushed the brake pedal, nothing happened. He was going too fast. He skidded off a cliff. The car turned over. The dream ended just before he hit the rocks at the bottom of the cliff.

He woke up sweating, his heart beating noisily in the darkness. He couldn't get back to sleep, even though he usually slept until about eleven on weekends.

As time went by memories of the dream faded. The excitement of the arrival of his new car grew.

It was a warm, sunny day. Marcus rushed into the agency, swinging the door into the wall, but his blood froze and he almost keeled over, gasping with fright as he saw the number plate - MJ21.

Emyr Wills-Wood (12)

The Vault

It was dark in the little town of Chippingham. A boy called Dom was on his way home from school. As he ambled home he turned a corner and heard a rustle in a nearby bush. He went to look at it and suddenly there was a bone-chilling click. Then the bush vanished. It was replaced by a dark hole. He had an hour until he had to be home so he went in. He fell. The walls were rough and thorny. Finally he hit the hard floor. He got up and limped to a door.

Inside the door was a sort of vault. It was empty and eerie. In the middle of the vault was a translucent figure plagued by scars and dents.

'Hello,' it said in a groaning tone of voice, 'you are Dom, right?' its voice echoing around the room. 'I'm called Scar, I was normal until a certain jewel resembling my life was removed from a table in a classroom. Do you know where it is?'

'No … I mean, yes. It as an accident. I kicked the jewel off the table.'

'Give it back.'

'OK.' He threw it out of his pocket and made for the door but tripped over a bump into a small metal cage.

Ten months later Dom's parents were still worrying in wailing fits of sorrow. They never found out about their son. Faraway their son was rattling on his cage.

Sina Yadollahi (12)

The Brown Lady

I was alone in the house. I was reading a book I had got on my previous birthday when I heard a creak on the stairs. I thought to myself, *it can't be the cat, she's outside,* so I put down my book and went to the stairs. There was nothing.

I went back to the living room and started to read again. *Creak!* I jumped with fright. When I had calmed myself down I went to the stairs to see what was there. There was nothing. I was scared as there was a creak on the same stair twice, but nothing was there. I decided to go into the kitchen to get something to eat. When I was walking back past the stairs they *creaked!* A chill rushed down my spine. I turned to look at the stairs and then sprinted to the living room.

I had seen a ghostly figure. It was a lady dressed in brown, but her face was blank.

She disappeared and never came back.

Amy Phillips (12)

Scary Story

Once on a very dark night when there was a full moon and wolves were howling, the phone rang. Vicky answered it. All she could hear was heavy breathing.

'I can see you,' a man whispered. Vicky stayed silent. 'Meet me by the bleeding tree in the grim woods at midnight tonight,' he said frighteningly. 'If you don't meet me I will haunt you for the rest of your life.' He hung up.

That night she waited at midnight whilst the wind was blowing and the owls were hooting. In the distance she could see an old house with a man standing in front of it. She wondered what he was doing. The man started to walk towards her. Suddenly he got nearer and nearer until he reached her.

'I asked you to meet me,' he said.

'Yes,' answered Vicky shakily.

'Follow me,' the man said.

So Vicky did.

They were walking slowly towards the old house Vicky had seen in the distance. As they got closer she began to get more scared.

They walked into the old house. There was nothing inside at all, apart from one big yellow slide.

'Go to the top of the slide and slide all the way down,' the man said.

Vicky climbed all the way to the top and slid all the way down again. Then the man slid down.

He said to Vicky, 'Thank you for meeting me tonight. I just wanted to have some fun.'

Sophie Panagopoulos (12)

The Cleary Witch

A long time ago there was an old woman who lived in an old house. She stared out of her window waiting for her next patient to knock at the door. The lady was called Agatha Cleary. She was a herbalist and very clever.

There had been many suspicions that Agatha was a witch, but nothing was proven. Every time people took her remedies, they died. The officers of the law came to Agatha's house because there had been so many deaths. She would have to go on trial for being a witch.

Agatha left her house and walked to the Court House. She went inside and stood there. The people snarled and sneered at her. They sat her in the ducking stool. As she looked down at her reflection in the water a tear dropped from her eye. The man pulled the lever and splash - she was dead.

Agatha had a greedy sister called Martha. She heard of Agatha's death and went straight to claim her house. She opened the door. Agatha appeared and shouted, ' Get out of my house!' Martha tried to run out but she was never seen again.

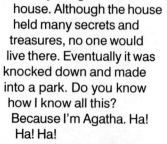

Some say she ran away, others say that she was killed. Many reported scary things at the house. Although the house held many secrets and treasures, no one would live there. Eventually it was knocked down and made into a park. Do you know how I know all this? Because I'm Agatha. Ha! Ha! Ha!

Clare Dunderdale (9)

Dares

There was a house that stood on Pringle Hill. Mine and Kara's dare was to spend the evening at the weirdo's house. The weirdo was a 95-year-old woman that wouldn't let anyone pass her house.

We stood at the huge metal door. *Knock! Knock! Knock!*

The door creaked open and she stood there before us - 'the weirdo'.

'What do you want?' spat the old lady.

'We need some answers for our history project,' I said.

Me and Kara followed her in. It was so cold we could see our own breath.

'Wait here,' muttered the old woman.

Kara and I were all alone.

'Let's explore while she's gone,' Kara whispered. Then we both headed up the huge, dark staircase. There were footsteps following behind us. We turned to look but there was no one. I could feel heavy breathing on my neck. We sprinted to the top of the stairs.

We entered a room and in front of the window was a rocking chair. The chair was going back and forth. Both of us gasped. In the chair was the old lady. She was dead. We screamed and ran down the stairs and didn't stop until we reached my house. The police came immediately.

Later that evening the police came to thank us. The woman had been dead for over 3 weeks …

Lucy Blower (11)

Tragedy Strikes

Some people say your childhood is meant to be the most enjoyable part of your life. For me it was the worst part of my life.

It all started when my parents decided it would be a good idea to go for a trek. I knew they were trying to avoid the fact that it was raining heavily.

Ever since my little brother had died they didn't have any time to cuddle me. I knew I was a big boy because I was nearly seven, but I still needed some cuddling. My parents were being really horrible to me lately. I think they were really shocked about my brother's death and were trying to find a reasonable explanation. But I knew …

It was all because of me. My brother was really ill and I had to feed him his medicine, but I'd had other stuff to do.

Ahead of me stood a cold, gloomy, dark church. My parents were miles back so I stepped into the church. My footsteps echoed throughout the hall There was suddenly a long cry. Immediately I heard little children's voices. I stepped back out, but I was no longer on the trek path, I was in a graveyard. Starving vultures stared at me like I was food to feast on.

Suddenly I saw my brother's dead body, his cute little fingers twitched. I ran through the church door. All that there was was my brother's toy covered in blood lying on the floor.

Ben Araya (11)

The Haunted House

It was a dark, scary night on Hallowe'en, the full moon was out and wolves were howling.

The moon shone down on two young boys both aged nine. Their names were Patrick and Danny. Patrick was dressed up as Dracula. He had dummy teeth and fake blood dripping from his mouth. Danny was dressed up as a ghost.

They had gone out trick or treating. When they were on their way home they decided to take a short cut through the graveyard. Patrick saw through the mist an old, deserted house with a smashed window covered with a spider's web.

Patrick said to Danny, 'I dare you to go into that old, scary house.'

Danny replied, 'Only if you go in with me.'

So they both snuck up to the small brown door. When they reached the door it blew open with a squeak. They slowly walked in, the door closed on them and they quickly turned around and, to their horror, the door wouldn't open. They made their way to see if there was a back door. On their way they saw an old door so they decided to take a look inside. Opening the door they saw two skeletons hanging on hooks and they started screaming. Then a bat appeared and chased them. The two boys, with their hearts pounding, found a way out and sprinted home.

From then on the two boys swore that they would not cut through the graveyard ever again.

John G MacDonald (10)

The Haunted House

One bright spring day on Summerfield Road there was no sign of movement apart from two little children, one 9 and the other 8. They were wandering the street shouting at each other when they heard someone screaming, *'Argh! Help!'*

'What was that?' cried Sam, who was the 8-year-old.

'I don't know,' replied John in a scared manner.

'It's coming from old Marge's house across the road from our house,' exclaimed Sam loudly.

'Let's go check it out,' said John.

And they did.

They were at the door when they heard the scream again. *'Argh! Help!'*

They got a plant pot and smashed the door down to find it was already open. 'Old Marge, are you in here?' they both said hoping for an answer. There was no answer whatsoever. They searched downstairs and found nothing but a table leg from the kitchen. They sneaked up the stairs onto the landing. They crept across the dirty landing to a door and peered in. There was nothing there. They turned round and to their horror they heard something go, *'Boo!'*

As fast as their legs could carry them, they ran downstairs and out of the door.

The two boys who searched that house were never heard of again. From that day onwards the house was called 'The Haunted House'.

Matthew Allott (8)

A Ghostly Moment

On one mysterious, spooky evening at Longingtons young William Watson was out of his bed again. The gloomy lights began to fade and the night was still. Most students would have just stayed in bed and done as they'd been told, but not William, he always had to be different. Like he always said, 'Be your own person, don't be a sheep and follow the crowd'. He always knew that what he said obviously didn't appeal to many people because they never listened.

He appeared to leave the school through the back door. Peter Preston had dared him to do it. But this time it was worse.

He was going to the old potting shed, which the older kids often told stories about it being haunted. He knew that they obviously weren't true.

When he got to the bottom of the school's garden he caught a glimpse of a rickety old building. As he opened the door, inside, it was dark and damp with the stench of decomposed plants. All of a sudden the door slammed shut behind him. William tried to open the door but he knew for sure that he was trapped. Fear began to run through his veins as he heard the door being tried from the outside. It silently creaked open and there, through the shadows, stood the outline of a bony figure leaning against the doorway. It didn't take him long to find out that it was his late grandfather, Albert Watson - that didn't half freak him out!

Charlotte Forster (10)

The Haunting Cry

There once was an eight-year-old girl called Elizabeth who lived with her grandma and grandad. They had a very nice life living in a huge, ancient mansion until one night when Elizabeth was awoken and heard a muffled voice whispering her name. 'Elizabeth, Elizabeth.'

She went up the old, crumbly stairs to the attic to see who was making the haunting cry. She silently opened the attic door and peered in. She saw a ghostly shadow sweep across the floor as she stepped back in horror. She then gave a startled scream as she saw her grandma and grandad lying there on the floor. 'Noooo!' she screamed.

'Darling, Darling, what's wrong?'

'Oh!' sighed Elizabeth silently. 'It must have been a nightmare.'

She looked around the room expecting to see her grandparents but she saw nobody standing there ...

Ellen Jones (10)

The Weeping Doll

'I hate it! I hate it!' Susan yelled. 'I never wanted to move her in the first place.'

'Stop it Susan for goodness sake. I only wanted to move here because it was where I grew up,' her mum shouted.

Susan cried herself to sleep that night, that was until suddenly she heard someone else weeping. At first she thought nothing of it, but it came back every night. Susan could stand it no longer. She took her lamp and followed the weeping down the corridor where she found herself in front of the cupboard under the stairs. In she clambered and to her astonishment the crying seemed to be coming from a small porcelain doll. 'Oh dear,' Susan whispered. She carried the doll carefully up to her room where she put her on her window ledge.

The next morning Susan woke up remembering the events of the night before. At breakfast she decided to tell her mum her story.

'Come here Susan,' replied her mum after Susan had told her the tale. 'I promise to tell you about the doll tonight if you don't argue for one whole day.'

'OK,' answered Susan.

That night Susan sat on her mum's lap waiting for the story. 'Here goes,' said Susan's mum. 'When I was little my sister died of a disease. My mum took a doll out of my sister's collection as a memorial, but her ghost still comes back weeping to warn people that soon something terrible will happen ... argh!' ...

Colette Barker (10)

The 'Haunted' House

The wind was howling, the moon was round and shiny and it was Hallowe'en.

In a small village of Snuggleton-upon-Scare three best mates were out trick or treating. Dressed as a spider was Jo-Jo, the oldest. Ellie, the youngest, was dressed as a witch with a cat sewn onto her pointed hat. Tom was Ellie's brother but never acted like one. He was wearing a neon skeleton outfit.

It was just striking nine o'clock as the children arrived at the last house. Mrs Rolind was a widow; she lived alone at the edge of the village. She was thought to be the oldest living resident of the village and knew everything. There was a shabby-looking house a few minutes walk along the lane. No one knew much about it and never wanted to for some weird reason.

As the children entered the house they asked her about the old house down the lane. She told the children to investigate with a freaky grin on her face. The children thanked her and left, confused about the grin.

When the children arrived at the house, Ellie opened the door, *creeak!* Everybody got the chills. *Dong!* Ellie gave a shrill scream. It was only the town hall clock striking ten, only it sounded different.

And then a hand tapped Ellie on the shoulder. 'Stop it Tom!' commanded Ellie.

'But it's not us,' chorused Tom and Jo-Jo together.

'Then who is it?' asked Ellie turning round …

Anisha Meggi (12)

Spooked!

I sat in my room. Mum was out. I hadn't seen her for days, but before she left she had been crying. I was stuck in this old dump by myself.

I hated this house. When mum and dad split up me and mum moved (6 years ago). I hated it. The only reason we bought this 2,000-year-old house was because of the size - it was a castle, with balconies and stuff - it was dirt cheap cos it was rumoured to be haunted. I don't believe that, I'm 18, not a kid.

Suddenly a load of ghostly figures appeared around me. They had come the other day. I felt a chill go down the back of my neck. Evil grins spread across their evil faces. They came towards me and a few swept right through me. I went cold all over. A lady dressed up in a Victorian dress came towards me. I walked back and I suddenly was on the slippery balcony.

Her arms stretched out and pushed me in the chest. Once again I was over the edge of the balcony. I screamed loudly. I fell for what seemed a lifetime, then hit the gravel outside. I didn't feel a thing. I looked at my hands, they were a ghostly white, then I remembered what had happened at school. No one had seemed to see me. I suddenly realised why Mum had gone off crying, why no one could see me - I was a *ghost!*

Helen Hawcroft (10)

A Cold Night

It was a cold and rainy night and there was a chill in the air. Emma had just finished a day of school and had passed the graveyard. You see, her mother had just died and Emma was very upset. She decided to go to the graveyard and see her mother's grave.

Emma started to cry but suddenly she heard this terrifying groaning noise, 'Emma, Emma.' It went quiet, she began to tremble. She ran and ran but kept seeing misshapen figures. She thought, *no, it can't be a ghost!*

Emma could hear her heart thumping, then suddenly she fell into a grave and the second she touched the floor she woke up. She jumped up to find herself not in the grave but on the wet grass.

She thought it was a dream but she was wrong. Emma knew it was getting late and her dad would be wondering where she was, so she quickly rushed to the gate to find that she had not opened the gate but her hand had gone straight through.

She looked down at her body. It was a gruesome white figure. She was a ghost! She could see her dad walking to her saying, 'Where have you been?' But then all he heard was a faint scream and she disappeared.

Harriett Monaghan (12)

Axed

Beatrice was playing in her garden when she stumbled on an old grave. She had been told never to go near this part of the garden but wasn't sure why. Up until this day she had been a carefree, happy little girl.

It was whilst eating tea that Beatrice first saw it - a spine-chilling ghost standing at the door. It had two bright red eyes, a ragged coat and wore hob-nailed boots. It had a horrific scar across its left cheek and carried an axe. It walked up to her father, raised its axe above its head but then it disappeared. Beatrice hadn't had the breath to scream, and it was obvious her parents couldn't see this blood-curdling ghost. She tried to put the thought out of her mind but a fortnight later she saw the ghost again at her bedside and it began talking to her in a low, gruff voice. It was telling her to kill her beloved parents. There was nothing she could do; this petrifying ghost was controlling her. She walked into her parents' room in a trance carrying her parents' gun. Beatrice emerged, dragging the bodies into the bathroom where she filled the bath with acid and dissolved the bodies.

Beatrice later committed suicide, too distraught to live with the fact that she'd murdered her parents.

Nobody ever found out who committed the murders but rumour has it Beatrice's ghost still haunts little innocent girls to this day.

James Kirk (12)

For No Particular Reason

It was a dark, cold night. The air was clear, the wind howled. For no particular reason Sally felt nervous. She waved her parents, Mr and Mrs Lewis, off at the door. Sally noticed there was no moon in sight. She had to go out and collect leaves she needed for studies. She wrapped up warm and ventured into the park, daring not to go too close to the graveyard. She bent down to collect the leaves and dropped her torch. It rolled onto a large stone jutting out. Sally felt cold. She turned, feeling something tapping her shoulder. Nothing was there. She picked up her torch, the battery was fading. She noticed writing on the stone. She dusted off the cobwebs and years of debris. 'RIP Sally Lewis' it read, '1809'.

She stumbled back. Could that be possible?

All around her she could feel someone tapping her shoulder, wrapping their arms around her. She turned and ran. She ran for her life. She entered her street and ran straight home, locking the door. She ran to bed and hid under the covers. Suddenly there was a tap on the sheet. She slowly pulled her sheet down to see that it was *Mrs Lewis …*

Ellie Cook (11)

Annabell's Ghost

It was a dark and gloomy night with a full moon and Ellie had just moved to her new house, or should I say castle, that her parents had inherited from her great grandmother Annabell.

Ellie was staring out of the old, rickety window listening to the wind screaming, wondering if it was the wind screaming at all. Her eyes gazed down and looked at her graveyard garden. Just then the clock struck two. In fact, all the clocks did and it was only 5pm. Ellie then felt an earthquake sort of feeling. With her heart pounding she looked down at the graveyard and saw ghosts rising from every grave.

She screamed at the top of her voice and by doing so, attracted the attention of one ghost. That ghost turned and looked at her and then, with a screeching sound, flew towards her and grabbed the necklace around her neck. That necklace was a locket and inside it was a picture of Annabell.

The necklace opened and the ghost got sucked in and then it shut.

Now when Ellie sleeps at night at 2am the locket shakes and the ghost of Annabell tries to break free and when people ask Ellie if she's OK about her great grandmother dying, she smiles and says, 'Yes because I've got her right here with me,' and holds the locket tight in her hand.

Hollie Goman (11)

A Soldier's Tale

It was the 23rd December 1983, the night was cold and there was a storm brewing in the west. Everyone was asleep in the army camp in Washington apart from one man, Sergeant Max Hann. Max paced round his bland room. He was restless, he didn't know why, but an hour or so later he too collapsed on his bed and slept.

It was about 12pm and he was awoken by a loud splashing sound from outside. He slowly got out of bed, still half asleep, and peered out of his grey curtains to see only the same dull view. He saw nothing unusual so dawdling back to his cold bed fell back to sleep.

A few hours later Sgt Max Hann woke up again because of another even louder sound. This time he decided to take action. Max got up again, this time more alert, and looked out of the window. He started to turn around to go back to bed but just as he did, out of the corner of his eye, he saw a streak of blue. Max pivoted around to see a drowning body shouting for help, men laughing and watching as it did.

'Hey,' shouted Max, 'for goodness sake help him.' But the pale figures carried on.

Suddenly, one after the other, the figures faded away. *Must have been imagining it,* thought Max, *at least whatever they were, they have gone now* - or have they?

Sara Griffiths-North (11)

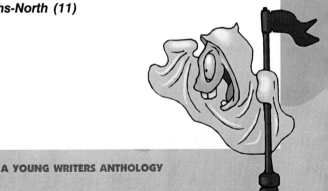

The Dark Lane

'These boxes are so heavy,' cried the man, putting them in the removal van.

Megan and her mum and dad were moving to the country. Megan, who was twelve, didn't really want to go. She didn't want to leave her school and her friends behind.

'We won't be far away from all your friends,' said her mum. 'You can still see them whenever you like.' It was only a couple of miles away, but to Megan it seemed like a hundred miles.

They got in the car and followed the removal van. When they got to the new house, they started unpacking. They finished the unpacking and Megan was bored. 'Can I go around to Lisa's house?' she asked her mum.

'No darling, not today, we've just moved in.'

Megan was upset and started arguing with her mum.

That night when everyone was in bed, Megan thought of a plan. She packed her bag and left the house. She started walking to Lisa's house.

It was very dark outside and there were no stars out. It was a bit foggy, and Megan was scared. She carried on down a narrow lane. She saw shadows and thought she heard screams, but she could have been imagining them.

When she got to Lisa's house it was midnight. She threw stones up to Lisa's bedroom.

'What are you doing here?' asked Lisa in surprise.

'Let me in,' said Megan.

In Lisa's house Megan couldn't sleep. Mum and Dad would be worried about her. She had better go home. She didn't want to wake Lisa up again, so she quietly left the house and started to walk the two miles home.

She heard the noises again in the dark lane and the screaming sounds. She thought someone was following her, but carried on walking quickly. Suddenly she stopped dead still and turned around. Nothing was there so she turned back again. She gasped as she saw the ghost in front of her. It was a very old man with a long beard and carrying a walking stick. He was shaking the walking stick at her. Megan ran around him and didn't stop running until she got home.

She let herself into her house and crept upstairs to bed. Mum and Dad hadn't even noticed she was gone. They were fast asleep.

In her bed she couldn't stop thinking about the old man, but she drifted off to sleep.

In the morning she decided to tidy her new bedroom and put all her toys away. She opened the drawer of an old cupboard that had been left in the house and looked inside. It was very dusty, but at the back she could see something. She reached out and grabbed it quickly. She brushed off the dust and saw that it was an old photograph. It was the old man with the long beard standing in the garden of her new house.

She dropped her teddy and ran downstairs. Her mum and dad were eating hot buttered toast for breakfast.

'Look at this. I found it in the drawer.'

Her dad looked at the photo closely. 'This is Mr Bailey who used to live in this house ten years ago,' he said. 'He died here, but people say that he walks down the dark lane at night. It's just a made up story of course!'

Megan carried on staring at the picture while she went into the living room. She never told her parents what she had seen that night, but would never walk down that dark lane again.

Lindsey French (11)

The Dead Tower

This story is one to be told to the strongest of minds as none live who remember this tale.

It all started one stormy night in a dark and evil forest. Four explorers named Gareth, Rex, Max and Hector marched through the trees for what seemed like an eternity until a small light emerged at the end of the trees - a wisp. The explorers began to follow the wisp as if hypnotised by its intriguing glow. They were led across a rickety bridge that swung violently to a tower that spiralled up into the sky. The wisp beckoned them into the dimly lit tower they immediately obeyed.

In a flash the wisp, with an evil laugh, disappeared. The party snapped out of their trance as the lights flickered out. The party panicked and stood back to back. A voice boomed out of the darkness shaking the walls and two massive eyes appeared from the gloom.

'Foolish mortals! I will never understand why you are all so possessed by bright lights. Now because of your mistake you will all die!'

The door slammed. A cold draught filled the room and the lights flickered back on. Corpses lay across the floor and began to rise. Zombies!

The explorers were petrified, they didn't move, or breathe. The zombies advanced and one by one raised their bloodied claws and struck them all down.

Screams echoed through the forest as another gang of explorers entered a dark and evil forest.

Mitchell Wakeman (11)

Living On

'My parents are going to kill me!'

'Mine too. I can hear them now, a 12-year-old out at 11, it's not safe!'

'Oops, help me up, I'm stuck.'

'Catch me if you can.'

'No, come on, help me up, argh …'

'No, no, wake up, wake up.'

These are the type of 'visions' Tracey had been getting ever since her mother, Daisy, had died two years ago. But to her they felt like memories but Tracey had neither seen nor heard of these girls before. Lately these had been getting clearer and clearer.

She had told her dad many times, but her mother had complained of seeing these too, so he just thought it was a way of holding on to her dead mum, after all she was only 8 when she had died.

'Trace, are you ready to go to school?'

She hesitated to tell him about the 'dream' as he called them. 'Yeah Dad, just coming,' she said, deciding not to tell him just yet. 'Bye Dad, see you later,' she said trying to make herself smile.

'Is there something on your mind Trace? I know it's three years since Mum died tomorrow but …'

That had struck a nerve. Tracey burst out crying. 'Oh Trace, don't start crying, you've got to go to school.'

Tracey went very rigid in her dad's arms.

'Daisy, don't let me die, don't let me die.'

'I won't, I won't. Hello, I'd like an ambulance please, my friend's just been hit by a car.'

'Trace, Trace wake up. Tracey please wake up,' he was sobbing hard. He had already lost his wife, was he going to lose his daughter too? Were all the things she had said true? They sounded so much like Daisy. Why hadn't he believed her? All these things went round and round his head.

'David, I'm so sorry but Daisy had it coming to her. She left me for dead. She made sure I could never get married, have children or grow old. I never ever got to see my 12th birthday because of her all because of her. I hate her. She said she wouldn't let me die and she did. I hate

her! I really hate her! Tracey had to go too. She's dead. I killed both of them and now I'm going to kill you. Don't worry Tracey died of shock and you'll die of a heart attack.'

David felt sharp stabbing pains going up his left arm. He looked down at Tracey took one last breath and …

Josie Philp (12)

The Ghost With A Broken Heart

The pub was a wonderful place. It had crocuses, honeysuckle and a cherry tree. It was made of old yellow stone and had a thatched roof. It was also very old, about 300 years old.

The people who owned it were called the Humphreys. They were happy, hilarious people who made you feel comfortable when you were around them.

However, their pub was not as it seemed. In their pub there was something lurking in every room.

One cold, frosty Christmas a girl called Rosie Humphreys was asleep dreaming of Christmas trees, wrapping paper and Christmas turkey. Suddenly she awoke and was sure that something was in her room. She sat up straight and stared at a figure that was dressed in Victorian clothes, all black with a black bonnet.

In the morning Rosie woke up and said to herself, 'Was it a dream?' She got out of bed, slipped her dressing gown on, put on her slippers and sleepily walked downstairs. She thought maybe she could do some research, but before she did she needed to get dressed.

Later, she was at the local library doing her research and found out that the girl who visited her was called Elizabeth Howard. She had lived in the pub years ago and perhaps she had come back because she had some unfinished business. Now Rosie had enough research, she now knew what to do. She would wait for Elizabeth to visit her again and would try to help her.

That night when she was sleeping she heard a noise, sat up and questioned, 'Are you Elizabeth?'

Then a gloomy voice repeated back and said, 'Yes I am and are you Rose?'

'Yes, that's right, I'm Rose,' she said cheerfully. Rose carried on, 'Elizabeth, how can I help you?'

Elizabeth told her that she fell in love with a boy called Fred. One day Fred disappeared and she had no idea what happened to him and she couldn't leave the pub until she knew what had happened to him.

Rosie remembered that when she was doing her research she'd read about a boy called Fred who had drowned in the lake.

So Rosie broke the news to Elizabeth. Elizabeth cried and as Rosie went to give her a big hug she vanished from her arms.

Sophie Williams (10)

Simon's Scary Birthday

Simon was a boy who liked playing and hated school. He was turning fourteen; he wanted to go to a haunted house for his birthday. Simon sent out his invitations to his friends but he only got one reply and the fair was leaving soon. Simon decided to go to the fair.

On his birthday he charged into the fair with his friend Ted. As they went in the doors slammed shut. 'Welcome to my haunted fair,' laughed a mysterious voice.

'I've got a great idea, let's go and meet in thirty minutes,' snapped Simon.

'OK!' Ted replied.

They ran off in different directions.

Ted went on the roller coaster. 'Wahoooo, this is fun!' Ted shouted. Ted also found a haunted house with a brass door. 'Yes, a haunted house, just what I came for.' Ted's eyes lit up. He crept in …

'Welcome to my *House of Doom*,' laughed the mysterious voice.

The door shut with a thud.

'This isn't scary,' Ted yawned, then he saw it, a machine which was very rusty. It was called the 'Zapper Test'. 'It's a quiz, I love quizzes,' Ted whispered to himself.

He had to answer the question, 'Who writes the series Goosebumps?'

'… R L Stine!' *Bzzz,* in two seconds he was thin air.

Later, Simon was searching for Ted. 'Ted, Ted …' Simon called.

Suddenly monsters jumped out from nowhere. A few seconds later they swallowed Simon.

Andrew Wu (9)
XII Apostles RC Primary School, Leigh

The Haunted Dress

When Maisy stumbled up the dull grey path a mixture of excitement and nerves filled her body.

The land was desolate and the hill on which the house was built was a mass of blackness.

As she approached the window she noticed an old woman perched on a rocking chair.

'You'll be fine with Mrs Taylor won't you?' Mum asked Maisy.

'Yes, Mum,' Maisy replied, as she walked through the cobwebs on the rickety, rotten door.

'See you on Monday darling. Love you!' Mum called as she turned and disappeared slowly.

'Come in dear,' said an ancient voice in the distance.

Maisy peered around the edge of the door.

'Don't be shy pet. Your bedroom is to the left, at the top of the landing. Now up you go.'

With that she tiptoed up the stairs, but instead of turning left she turned right and ventured through a small white door.

In the room, hung in the corner was an old lace Victorian dress. The only other thing in the room was a small mahogany box. As Maisy opened the lid of the box music played so sweetly, and in the corner of her eye she spied a whirl of movement. She turned around to find the dress was waltzing around the room.

'Argh!' Maisy screamed as the window slammed shut.

Suddenly the dress stopped moving and silence filled the room once again.

'What's the matter?' shouted Mrs Taylor, rather startled.

'The dress was moving on its own!' Maisy answered, with a trembling voice.

'I don't know, what a vivid imagination you young ones have! Come on, let's go and get a drink of hot chocolate before bedtime!'

Rhiannon Hayes (10)
XII Apostles RC Primary School, Leigh

Bingo

One stormy night her door swung open, she hid under her bed and she saw a pair of green, rotten, hairy feet. She grabbed her torch, she tried to find the switch, when she found it she turned it on but the feet were gone. She laid in bed thinking about what she'd seen. *How did it get in?* she thought suspiciously.

Soon it was morning, she told her mum but her mum told her to stop telling lies. Her mum got her school stuff ready, then she went to school.

She went into the girls' bathroom, she took out her note pad and pencils and drew the feet to try and convince everyone. Before she could tell anyone the monster came in her toilet and she screamed until her voice was gone, but no one heard her. Soon her light went out.

No one saw that poor girl again or the green, rotten, hairy-footed monster again.

Jemma-Lee Greensmith (11)
XII Apostles RC Primary School, Leigh

The One Minute Quest

Once upon a time a girl called Mia was walking her dog in the forest. She fell in a trapdoor. 'Help!' she shouted. Her dog started to bark. 'Shhh we will have to find our own way out,' whispered Mia. Someone tapped her on the shoulder. 'Argh!' Mia screamed. 'A ghost!'

She carried on walking and she came to a door. She went to the door but the door was locked. She heard a voice. The voice said, 'This door leads back into the forest. You must go and search all the rooms and doors for the key. You have to get a key in one minute or else I will eat you because I am getting hungry. Your time starts … now! Hurry I am starving!'

Mia was so scared she ran off not thinking where she was going. She went into the room. It had a question in it, there was a button, she pressed it.

The voice said, 'If you answer the question you receive a key.'

'I'm really scared,' whispered Mia.

'Question time,' said the voice. 'Where does the Queen live?'

'Buckingham Palace,' answered Mia.

'Correct,' said the voice.

Her vision started to fade. 'It was only a dream!' shouted Mia.

Her mum turned round … *she was a skeleton!*

Rachel Davies (9)
XII Apostles RC Primary School,
Leigh

Aqua's Spooky Tail

Once upon a time there was a girl called Aqua, a normal girl with a normal life, but Aqua had a vivid imagination. She had nightmares every night, one night her dream came true. This is her story …

'Mum,' I said, 'I've had a bad dream.'

'Come here then,' Mum said.

I was too scared to get out of my bed in the night. 'Mum I can't come I'm too … er. I'm OK,' I shouted to Mum.

'*I'm coming*,' screeched Mum. She sounded like a zombie.

'Argh!' I screamed.

'You're dead!' said Mum.

'I'm gonna chop your head off … oh yeah,' Dad moaned.

'What's happening?' I cried.

'Chop! Chop!' Dad moaned.

'No it's a dream!'

Bang! I'm in my bed again, it was a dream. 'Mum! Mum!' I shouted.

'*I'm coming*,' shouted Mum.

Oh no she sounded like a zombie. *Chop!* Mum's head flew off and in my lap.

'Aqua!' said the head.

'Argh!' I threw her head off my lap. 'Argh!' *Chop!* My head flew off and it flew to the North Pole and froze!

My dad woke me up, it was a dream. But the next night, I had the same dream ... this might mean something. I still don't know where Mum is.

Watch out! If you read this story your head may be chopped off! *Ha! Ha! Ha! Ha!*

Milla Young (9)
XII Apostles RC Primary School, Leigh

Hallowe'en

It was the night before Hallowe'en and everything was quiet until 12.01am. Two creatures swept over the land and arrived at a hotel called 'The Headless Horseman'. A living, goo-like substance just slid under the door of the hotel, whilst a hooded man stood at the door, no face, just a dark, empty space where a face should be. The man entered as silently as an owl whilst the goo just slid in leaving a trail of sticky slime. Suddenly, a loud scream was let out by a guest.

'Help me. Somebody help!'

The barman woke up. In front of him was the gooey substance named Slime. Slime leapt forward at the barman and opened a mouth of evil filled with fangs, slime, blood and limbs. The barman suffered terrible wounds but was still alive. As for the man with no face, he is called the Invisible Man. He entered a room full of children, sleeping children. He had a plan. Whilst they were asleep, he tied the children to chairs and covered their mouths with Sellotape as well as putting a sock in them.

Luckily, an angry mob of people came to slay the Invisible Man and to wipe out Slime. Half of the mob searched one way and the other went the other way. A pitchfork was lit and burnt Slime to a crisp. As for the Invisible Man, he was stabbed right where his face was meant to be. The children were set free.

That was the last time the Headless Horseman Hotel celebrated Hallowe'en.

Andrew Ashley (10)
XII Apostles RC Primary
School, Leigh

Premonition?

Sweat was trickling down my brow. Late Saturday night, parents gone out, alone at home, reading a scary book - that was my predicament and, I had to admit, I was a little scared. Then - I heard three loud knocks on the door …

I sprang up, crept towards the door, slowly turned the knob, and swung it open - nothing. No one there. I laughed as I slammed the door shut. It was only a practical joke. Pesky prankster kid from next door, I reassured myself. I turned around, and then, once again - I heard three loud knocks on the door …

I jumped to the door this time. I was going to catch the prankster! I swung the door open - mistake. Big mistake. This was no kid I was dealing with.

The apparition, seven feet tall, holding a blood-crusted dagger, draped in black and with a hood covering his head, looked me straight in the eye. 'You're next,' he said in a hoarse voice.

I couldn't move. It was like I was transfixed to that spot with invisible chains.

Then he raised the dagger, and brought it plunging down towards my neck …

'Nooo!' I screamed, and - looked around. My eyes adjusted to the darkness, as I rubbed my neck. Then I laughed. I was in my room. It had all been a dream, just a dream! I sighed with relief, and it was at that very moment that - I heard three loud knocks on the door …

Jehan Katrak (11)
Bombay International School,
India

Ghosts, Ya Right

One morning Anisa awoke after having a bad dream about strange creatures. Sitting up she noticed a note pinned to her door. It read -

'Anisa, meet me at the cemetery tonight. Don't be late or you'll be sorry!'

Scared, she asked Sheila, her friend, to come along. As they searched the deserted cemetery, something grabbed their ankles. They tried to escape but the grasp tightened. Dodging the hands they tried to run. A man dressed in a black cloak appeared. He said, 'I was the one who put you to sleep and pinned a note to your door. I am here to warn you. Here are two simple riddles for your parents. I have cast a spell on them, if they can give the correct answer, they will remain humans or else they will turn into whatever they actually are.'

Anisa and Sheila saw the riddles. The first one read -

'A box without hinges, key or lid

Yet golden treasure inside is hid'.

Sheila shouted, 'It's an egg!'

The second one read -

'Thirty white horses on a white hill

They champ and stamp and then stand still'.

Anisa said, 'It's teeth!'

At home her parents failed to solve the riddles. They slowly started to fade away, and Anisa could see through them. In no time she realised that they were actually … ghosts!

'Now that she knows our secret, what should we do with her?' asked her mother with an evil laugh!

Neomi Sanghrajka (12)
Bombay International School, India

Ghost Story

It was take-off time of the Indian military aircraft. They say it was then that Inspector Rathore was telling an official, the legendary, but unspoken tale of an inspector, by the name of Late Harbhajan Singh. After hearing the tale the official did not believe it. He thought the whole tale was a figment of the imagination. He found it hard to believe that the folk living by Changu Lake would have faith in unexplained, phenomena and things like 'ghosts' …

The story goes like this … It was another chilly winter's morning, but who knew this day was going to be a grave? 4am, Sepoy Harbhajan Singh goes for his daily walk. 5am, appointed on the special duty of taking a round of the camp. 5.15, during the round, an ice block breaks off the mountain. 5.16, Sepoy Harbhajan loses his balance. In a fraction of a second, he falls 8,000ft down. 5.17, he lands into icy cold mountain water and is swept away. His remains are not found. But defying all practical logic it is as if Harbhajan Singh is still alive.

'Sepoy Harbhajan Singh has been promoted to chief officer,' the official declared. Imagine till today they yet promote him and pay him his salary. It is extremely spooky how when his clothes are kept out they get crumpled and dirty as if they have been worn. His food is eaten and his water is also drunk!

The power he has is so great that people who believe in him always succeed and people, like the official in the plane who don't believe in him;

well the officer's plane crashed, everyone survived except for him. So you can see what a great force he has. Well were these incidents a coincidence or does he really exist?

Miloni Kothari (12)
Bombay International School, India

A Ghost Story

Legend goes that Silverwood Forest was haunted by a girl who had been kidnapped and taken there. She tried to run away but got lost and died. She vowed to take revenge and from that day anyone who entered the forest never left. Every midnight you could hear her say, 'Who dares to enter my forest?' So nobody ever ventured in the forest.

But Maddy and Zoe didn't believe the legend. There was no such things as ghosts and they were sure of it. So to prove they were right, turning a deaf ear towards everyone's warnings, they set out towards the forest.

As they approached the forest darkness fell upon them. It was night-time and a silvery mist rested upon the forest. The trees themselves seemed to have spirits residing in them. Maddy and Zoe took a deep breath and entered the forest. Shivering with fear they walked through the forest. It was night-time, they were tired so they decided to go to sleep, hunting for the ghost could wait.

Late at night Maddy heard it, someone or something was saying, 'Who? Who?' Quickly she woke Zoe and quiet as mice they tiptoed out of their camp. Then they saw it, sitting on a branch a little away from the camp. It was glowing a pale white, but it wasn't facing them. It said, 'Who? Who?' again and turned its head. Maddy and Zoe screamed and it flew away! The ghost of an owl! Laughing Maddy and Zoe returned home with a tale to tell about the so-called haunted forest.

Shreya Shah (12)
Bombay International
School, India

The Ghost That Wasn't

We went on a vacation to an old village in England, in the middle of nowhere. Since there were no hotels, we managed to stay in an old mansion. My parents went out the first night, leaving me alone. I normally love being alone at home but the mansion frightened me. I refrained from pleading to my parents to stay, because I felt silly stopping them.

The grandfather clock struck nine, I was already feeling restless and unsettled; the book I was reading ended just as the grandfather clock struck twelve. I yawned and fell asleep.

Suddenly, I felt something cold on my hand. I stirred, and the feeling went away … again something wet and icy brushed against me and I jumped up with a scream, just in time to see a white thing rushing out the window! Now I was really scared; I hid myself under the cover hoping I had been imagining things, when the window shook again. I saw something move in the corner, and heard a whistle, which I hoped was the wind. I wanted to ignore it, but I knew it was the ghost the caretaker had spoken of!

Before I could stop trembling, I felt something cold on my hand again, except this time I heard a slurp and saw something white with shining eyes look straight at me. It hit me then! I quickly put the lights on, to be sure, but I was right. This was no ghost at all, just a little dog licking my hand!

Sahir Zaveri (12)
Bombay International School, India

Captured By The Evil

Long ago in a forest of the dead in the pale moonlight where nothing was visible, except a green, creepy, slimy figure, this thing walked up and down the forest haunting it. He carried a bag of bones and flesh in one of his hands. The villagers called him B3M which meant Big Bag Bone Master.

One day a boy named Martin thought he was capable. He wanted to teach B3M a lesson for all the bad he had done in his dead life. The boy got ready and went to the forest. When he reached it he looked around, his hands and legs were covered with goosebumps. Suddenly cold hands caught him and started pulling him. When the hands left Martin, Martin turned around and saw B3M.

Martin was scared, he never thought B3M would be so portly and frightening. B3M let out a wicked laugh. This made Martin more scared. He screamed but nobody came to the rescue. He screamed again *and* the more Martin screamed the louder B3M would laugh. Martin decided to run. As he almost entered the village he was disturbed.

Some villagers say they saw not one pair but many pairs of hands pulling Martin back into the forest. Some say they heard screams and cries at night. Beware Martin's or B3M's spirit is lingering around, it could be right next to you …

Aditi Shah (11)
Bombay International
School, India

It Happened One Night

It was a dark, stormy night. The lightning tore across the sky and for a split second, the dark outline of the old mansion shone.

Inside, little Matt was terrified and sobbing. It was his first night at his grandfather's house. He crept under the bed and hid, but soon, his sobs trailed off as he caught sight of a little boy playing with a golden bird. The boy smiled, held out his hand and beckoned for Matt to follow. After a moment's hesitation, Matt crept out. The boy ran up the rickety stairs into the tower with Matt at his heels. Stealthily, the boys climbed up the spiral stairs to the attic.

When they entered, Matt was spellbound! The attic was beautifully decorated with lots of toys. The children played happily and their loud chattering drifted into the night. Outside, the wind raged …

'Wake up little Matt! What are you doing in the attic?' said Grandfather, shaking him awake. Matt looked around bleary-eyed. Slivers of sunlight scattered all around the attic, pouring in through the attic's thick walls. Cobwebs hung on the walls and a musty smell greeted him. He was covered with dust.

Was it a dream? He brushed himself and followed his grandfather. Just as he was leaving, a shiny object caught his eye. He bent and picked it up. It was a golden bird! He clutched it in his hand and smiled. He knew that he had found a friend and wouldn't be lonely anymore …

Tanya Panicker (11)
Bombay International School,
India

Ghost Story!

One dark and stormy night, a guitarist finished playing at a concert and was returning home on a horse. The man and the house got sopping wet while looking for an inn in the woods.

Suddenly he saw a dim light in the distance. On nearing, he saw a shabby inn. The small, broken-down signboard read, *Spooks Inn*.

The guitarist asked the innkeeper for a room. The ugly, pock-mocked innkeeper denied, but offered a small, dingy room that was haunted. The guitarist didn't mind renting the room for a night as he proclaimed he didn't believe in ghosts.

That night as the man played his guitar, he heard a hoarse voice saying, 'I'm gonna getcha and I'm gonna eat ya.' He glanced at the room and continued playing. This happened once again and so this time the man shut the windows and latched the door. This did not stop the voice and it occurred repeatedly for an hour. Now the man got scared and he realised that the voice was coming from the cupboard in the corner of the room.

He slowly crept towards the cupboard with the guitar like a weapon. He slowly opened the door and saw … a small, greenish-coloured ghost with a big bulky nose, and lots of warts on his face. The ghost was sitting in the cupboard, digging his nose and desperately trying to remove snot, and mumbling to himself, 'I'm gonna getcha and I'm gonna eat ya.'

The ghost got scared and vanished into thin air … forever.

Jahnavi Shah (12)
Bombay International School, India

The Haunted Mansion

We got off the bus at Rina's new home, Petit Hall. The gates were sparkling gold. I thought they looked like the gates to Heaven!

We ran down the tree-lined avenue, excited to explore. The enormous main doors led to an even more spectacular hallway, lined with panels which had many portraits. Entering the room, I felt a million eerie eyes upon me!

The door in front led into the library. It was massive! I excitedly started looking around. As we stretched up to reach a higher shelf, suddenly the bookcase flipped and we were in a pitch dark passage.

'W-w-w-where are we?' The passage smelt musty and cobwebs covered most of it. At the end of the passage there was a dim light walking towards us. *Blam,* now it was in front of us. It seemed to have got to us without breaking a single cobweb. Up close we saw her face, her skin was wrinkled, her eyes - sunken like deep hollows and her hair, limp and grey.

'Come on children,' she said. Her voice sounded witch-like. We were too petrified to speak and followed like robots. She drifted through the wall to a damp, cave-like room. Her appearance looked scary, not sinister.

'It has been years since I've had company. I was left here during World War II, nobody realised. I died here and am now destined to stay here until my spirit fades away,' she cackled. 'Do you know how long I have been waiting for this moment? I need two live spirits to give my spirits to. I think you will do just fine.' She blew out the candle, leaving us in the darkness and cackled again.

Rea Malhotra Mukhtyar (11)
Bombay International School, India

A Ghost Story

Peter had nobody to play with. The boys who lived near him were either too young or too old. So he had to make up his own games. One day he would be a pirate, another day a pilot. One day while Peter was playing 'Astronaut in Orbit', he got a long way away from home.

It became dark, it began to rain. Peter saw a house in the dark. So he went up to the house and knocked, but there was no answer. The door was unlocked so Peter walked inside. He felt somebody behind him. It was a ghost. The ghost then spoke up.

'What are you doing here? This is no place for a boy alone.'

'I'm lost,' said Peter. 'What are you doing here?' Peter asked with curiosity.

'I'm here to guard the treasure,' said the ghost. 'I'll let you guess where it is.'

Peter tried many times but all in vain. He finally gave up and asked the ghost, 'Where is the treasure?'

The ghost coughed, 'I don't know, I was hoping you would remind me.'

'I must be getting home,' said Peter.

'Still raining,' said the ghost. 'Take the umbrella which is in the closet.'

Peter thanked the ghost and opened the umbrella. Out poured the treasure.

Peter counted the money. The ghost let him take one home as a souvenir. But on thinking it over, Peter decided he would not show it to anybody. He had had a wonderful adventure.

Alyzae Salim Merchant (12)
Bombay International School, India

The Friendly Ghost

One sunny day there was a ghost who lived in a haunted house and his name was Billy. He was a friendly ghost. The windows were smashed in the house and the roof was made out of straw. The door was made out of wood. The best thing he liked to do was take a bath because he liked the water a lot.

One day some people came to the house - they were going to live there forever. Now Billy could not take a bath anymore.

One night a boy was coming down the stairs and he saw Billy, he got scared but the boy became Billy's best friend. The boy's mum and dad did not know about the ghost, it was a secret because Billy did not want his mum and dad to find out. Billy had to hide from the boy's mum and dad all the time.

Billy was playing football with the boy and they had a bath. Billy was happy that he could have a bath again. Billy liked the boy and they lived happily ever after.

Zia Khan (8)
Broadhurst Primary School, Moston

The Dancing Ghosts With Flowers

In a dark, dark forest there was a mysterious house, it was spooky and scary. Me and Tim were afraid and terrified. We went to solve the mystery of what was inside the house.

There was a creaky floor. Cobwebs around the room, floorboards lifted up when you walked on them. There were dark shadows behind me and Tim. When we looked back we saw two dancing ghosts, they were dancing with flowers.

They got me and Tim to dance. We started to dance to the beat. When we were dancing the phone rang and when I picked it up it went dead. Then it rang again, so I picked it up and it went dead again. It rang for a third time so I picked it up and it went dead again, but then the ghosts told me and Tim it was them that kept ringing.

Me and Tim then went out of the house and walked home because we were annoyed with the ghosts playing tricks on us.

Faline Welsh (9)
Broadhurst Primary School, Moston

Mystery Gang

Long ago 5 people and a dog were looking for ghosts. The dog stopped because he saw glowing footprints, they started to follow the footprints and they saw a ghost skeleton. They ran as fast as they could but the ghost kept on chasing them. The gang hid somewhere and they made a plan to capture the ghost skeleton. Once they had done their plan, the ghost skeleton fell in the trap and the gang cheered.

After that, the ghost came back and he got their dog. He took the dog with him to his spooky mansion where the lighting had broken to make it look creepy. The dog started to play tricks on the ghost, when the ghost turned around the dog found a bucket of water and he poured it on the ghost. The ghost turned in to gunk and the gang found them and they started to cheer.

Salman Shaheen (10)
Broadhurst Primary School, Moston

The Friendly Ghost

I was in a haunted mansion and I started to wander around. All of a sudden I felt a breeze. I turned around but there were no windows or doors open. 'What was that?' I said to myself. My heart was beating fast. I carried on. Suddenly I stopped still in silence. I saw something move.

'Hi, my name is Sponger, do you want to be my friend?'

'Who are you?' I said shocked.

'I am Sponger the friendly ghost.'

'OK then,' I said happily.

Let's play hide-and-seek,' Sponger said.

So I went and hid.

'1, 2, 3, 4, 5,' Sponger shouted.

I hid in a larger cupboard where I found 3 mysterious ghosts. One was called Bean, one was called Potato and one was called Tomato.

They said, 'What are you doing?'

'I am playing hide-and-seek with Sponger,' I replied.

'Come with us, we will show you a good hiding place.'

So I went with them and they kicked me out. I went flying back home.

Jade Asha Cleasby (9)
Broadhurst Primary School, Moston

The Ghost Hunter

On one cold night there was a haunted house near an old cottage. There lived a girl there called Ashley Peacock. She is a ghost hunter, she's been hunting for many years. She was going to the haunted house but she was scared a little bit.

On another creepy night Ashley went to the haunted house. When she went in the house the door shut. She looked around the house, then she saw a shadow, a moving shadow. She was scared, there were cobwebs and mice crawling about the place.

She went upstairs, she saw a television working, no one had turned it on. 'Something strange is happening here.' She saw another shadow so she broke the shadows and it all disappeared.

A couple of days later she was tired but happy that she'd done the ghost good, he had gone back to where he belonged.

Jasmina Mujagic (9)
Broadhurst Primary School, Moston

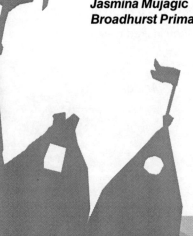

One Scary Night

I was on holiday when I went to a theme park. It was black, everyone was screaming so I went on six rides. Then I went on a scary ride and it broke down. It had loads of cobwebs and it was crooked. Then I heard a noise, it was like a noise that a ghost makes. I went to investigate.

When I was leaning on the wall it went through like a trapdoor. I looked round then the ghostly noise came from another direction so I went where I could hear the noise, but then I nearly fell so I caught two ropes and tried to get to the other side, and I made it.

I went on and some axes flew out but luckily they were only pretend. But suddenly someone or something started to sing. So I ran and hid for about 2 minutes. I came out and started searching again.

I heard someone shout my name so I quickly ran out, so I don't know if there was a ghost or not. When I went out there was no one calling my name so I went back in and there was a skeleton on the floor. I touched it and it was pretend so I carried on. Suddenly four different ghostly noises came from four different directions. I ran out screaming. Now no one will ever know if there is a ghost or not …

Rachel Cuncarr (10)
Broadhurst Primary School, Moston

The Spooky Haunted Mansion

One night in a faraway mansion there were rumours that people thought there was a ghost who was haunting the mansion. Some people said it was a ghost, some people said it was a fox but with bat wings; no one knew what it was. So people said, 'Call it a mystery.' People knew there was something in there because of the soggy footprints which led into the kitchen.

There were two boys called Kyle and Max. They went up to the mansion to see if the rumours were true. They had an investigation. They opened the door of the horrifying mansion. Once they got in the mansion they had a look around and they heard something moving, they went to have a look.

It was coming from the back room, they ran to the door and opened it but there was nothing there, it was weird. They turned round and checked all over but they still didn't find anything so they went home, but was there a ghost?

Before they got home their mum and dad were petrified and they never really knew if there was a real ghost. 'Ha, ha, ha!'

David Hilton (9)
Broadhurst Primary School,
Moston

The Ghost Friend

One morning, on Saturday, Ben and Sam were walking along the street when they saw a boy. Ben said, 'I dare you to say hello to the boy and say what is your name?'

Sam said, 'OK.' So Sam went over to the boy and said, 'Hello, what is your name?'

The boy said, 'Hello and my name is Billy.'

Sam said, 'Do you want to hang out with me and my friend Ben?'

Billy said, 'Yes of course.'

As they were walking down the street, Ben hurried to talk with Billy, so he faced Billy and it was like Billy had disappeared, he was nowhere to be seen, it was just Ben and Sam. The wind was blowing and the rain started and last of all was the lightning. The lightning started before the rain.

Sam and Ben went into their house because it had started to rain. After an hour it stopped raining. Sam and Ben were scared to go out. Billy knocked on the door for Sam and Ben. Sam and Ben went downstairs to see who it was. They opened the door and nobody was there. Billy was invisible and he went upstairs into Sam and Ben's room. Sam and Ben closed the door and went into their room, but Billy was up there . . .

Dervis Mujagic (10)
Broadhurst Primary School, Moston

The Evil Ghost

'Max I dare you to go down Horror Lane, then up the hill to Horror House,' said Paddy, giggling. 'Max are you doing the dare or are you scared?' Paddy said.

'No,' said Max, shaking.

'Chicken,' said Paddy.

'Shut up!' Max shouted.

'I'll come with you if you help me do my homework,' said Paddy.

'OK,' replied Max.

Slowly Max and Paddy crept down Horror Lane.

'Max look there is a ghost,' said Paddy.

'Where?' said Max.

'Only joking,' said Paddy. But there was a ghost following them.

Suddenly the ghost started to throw things and make scary noises. The boys started to shake and Max started to scream. Then the ghost picked Max up and threw him. Slowly Paddy walked to Max and they both ran to the hill, they ran over the hill to Horror House.

Slowly Max opened the gate and there was a ghost, an evil ghost. The ghost started to throw fireballs at them. They ran out of the gate, over the hill, out of Horror Lane.

Sadly Max and Paddy never went near Horror Lane again.

Michael Lawson (11)
Broadhurst Primary School, Moston

Ghost House

It was a cloudy night. John and Paul were walking down a dark street. It was freezing cold.

John said to Paul, 'Look at that house over there.' It was a deserted house whose curtains were flapping in the wind. Paul felt a chill running down his spine.

'Let's go and investigate,' said John.

Paul didn't know what he should do but he said, 'Okay then, I'll go with you in case you get scared.'

John stuck his tongue out at Paul. They both opened the door at the same time. It creaked loudly. There were cobwebs everywhere and the stairs looked as if they would collapse at any moment.

Paul was already scared to death.

John said, 'Let's go up the stairs to see what's there.'

'I don't think we should, John, our mums will be waiting for us,' Paul said nervously.

John didn't hear a word that Paul said because he was too busy climbing the stairs.

John and Paul reached the top of the stairs. They looked around; John saw a smashed photo, he picked it up. It was of a boy's face. To his horror, the boy in the photo opened his mouth and said, 'I don't like children because they killed me.'

Screaming with fright, John and Paul ran out of the house and never went back again!

Azeem Khan (10)
Broadhurst Primary School, Moston

The Empty House

Once there was a tall narrow house which rose before me in the shadows of the night. It was dark and cold and I was scared. I wondered if I should enter the empty house. After standing there staring up at the looming, dark, scary shadows, I realised I had to go into the house to get away from the cold night.

As I stepped into the house I could feel my heart pounding with fear. I looked around and saw that the house was old, with old-fashioned furniture and cobwebs everywhere.

I walked up the creaky, crooked stairs, as I got halfway up I heard a scream. I froze in terror and then an old grey lady surrounded by mist swooped past me. My heart jumped in fear.

I turned and ran down the stairs towards the door, only to be greeted by a headless horseman holding his head under his arm.

'Hello young lady,' he said. 'What brings you to the house on the hill?'

I screamed and ran past him through the door, to the echoes of laughter.

Then I felt something warm around my neck, it was my mum with her arms around me. It had all been a dream.

Robyn Leigh Phelan (11)
Broadhurst Primary School, Moston

Mysterious House

I looked in the sky and the sun was shimmering, suddenly I could smell something strange. It was a smell of musk that made me sneeze. Then the sky had just started to go gloomy and dull, I could hear a funny noise and see a mysterious shape.

I heard a creak and felt a shiver, I knew there was something going on but I didn't know what. I then heard another strange sound as I was trembling through fright.

As the mysterious shape came closer my mouth opened wider. All of a sudden, the wind grew stronger and a hailstone hit me. Then the mysterious shape faded and the sky went grey. I went home desperate to tell someone but I was just too scared in case something happened. My parents came home and the fright passed.

The next day I went back and nothing was there, the house was gone, the sky didn't turn dull, grey or moody and there was no my mysterious shape, so I gave a sigh of relief but I might have sighed a bit too soon. The mysterious shape appeared and said, 'I didn't mean to scare you, I was looking for a friend to talk to and I was wondering if you would be that person.'

'Of course,' I said.

He spoke to me about his problem, though it didn't seem to make sense. I went home forgetting about it all. He never came back until …

Sophie Phillips (11)
Broadhurst Primary
School, Moston

Spooky Streets

'Look at Spooky Street,' said John.

'Yeah, what about it? Are you scared?' replied Mark.

'Me, scared? I'm not scared of anything!'

'Prove it.'

John (the so-called daredevil) slowly crept down the street.

'I'll go … as long as you come with me.'

When they finally got to the bottom of the street, Mark noticed a strange mansion. 'Come on, let's go in.'

Slowly the two friends walked in. 'We need to stay together,' Mark whispered in a strange voice …

'OK.' John turned around and in Mark's place was a little girl. She started to cry and she was talking about a stick man. (She was about 3 years old.)

'Boo!' yelled Mark, trying to scare John. Mark turned back at John.

'You're not scary.'

All the excitement had caused Mark to forget about the girl and when he remembered he ran home like a shot.

'Mum do you know anything about that strange mansion on Spooky Street?'

Mum took a long time to answer, but in the end she said that about 12 years ago a little girl lived there and had got beaten up by a man with a stick. She'd been seriously beaten up and was scared for the rest of her afterlife . . .

Nathan Johnson (10)
Broadhurst Primary School, Moston

Ghost

'Ugh, look at that ugly house.'

'Yeah, it's like a pigsty.'

'I dare you to go and take a look through the window.'

'Would you?'

'I'll come with you.'

'OK.'

John and Fred walked up to the house. They both got shivers up their spines as they opened the gate. The path had little cracks in it. It looked like they were going to open and let you fall into Hell.

'I dare you to go and take a look or are you too scared?'

'No way. I'm not scared and I'll take a look but I bet you won't!'

'Oh yes I will, you watch!'

Fred opened the door and a wildcat that had no hair ran and pounced onto his knee. When we finally got it off he had a look inside. Then John shut the door on him and held it shut. He then ran down the path and hid behind the wall.

John stayed there for about ten minutes and then finally got up. He walked up to the house. John opened the door and shouted, 'Fred! Fred! Where are you?' There was no answer. He looked around and then he saw a shadowy figure.

It jumped at him and said with a mean voice, 'Ha, ha, ha my lunch.'

John staggered out. 'D-do y-you know where my friend is?'

'Yes I do actually.'

'Please can you tell me?'

'Yes, he ran out the back door and said there will be another boy coming in and now I can eat you!'

'No! Please don't!'

'Any last words?'

That moment Fred came with a piece of wood. He tried to hit the ghost but when he did John disappeared …

Alexander Colclough (10)
Broadhurst Primary School, Moston

Jasper And Jen

It was just yesterday that I was minding my own business at the dinner table inside a hotel when I closed my eyes and saw a ghost. It was small, grey and looked very cute, it also had blue eyes. It was floating around in the air like a kite without a string. I opened my eyes to see an empty dinner table.

Everyone and everything had gone, except mine. It was really weird. I closed my eyes and I saw the ghost again, it started talking to me.

'My name is Jasper and I am ten.' He didn't ask my name. Jasper starting talking again. 'I am a boy, I have a twin sister, her name is Jen. She should be here any minute now to meet you, you'll like her!' Jen sounded nice.

Someone shouted, 'Incoming,' from a distance! *Whoosh!* Another ghost appeared. It was Jen. She was the double of Jasper.

'Hey,' said Jen quite determinedly.

'Hello,' I replied.

They gave me a little bottle and told me to drink it, so I did. Suddenly I floated up in the air beside them.

'Follow on,' said Jasper, so we did. We went higher in the air as we started flying. We saw clouds everywhere, it was cool.

Finally we landed on ground. 'Where has the flying drink gone?' I asked.

'You've still got some, but don't waste it,' answered Jasper.

We were in an empty place.

'Where are we?' I asked.

'You'll see,' replied Jen . . .

Shelley McLachlan (10)
Collydean Primary School, Glenrothes

A Ghost Story

An old man called Jim moved into a haunted house. The house was big and old-fashioned. No one had lived there for 150 years. When he had unpacked he heard noises so he opened the back door and the noises stopped.

He said, 'Oh it must have been the birds.' He went back inside. He thought, *oh well I'll just go for a lie down.*

The ghost thought, *this is my chance to kill him. I will have the whole house to myself again.*

Suddenly the ghost went to suffocate Jim but the ghost's hands just went right through Jim's face. The ghost thought, *how will I kill him now?* He said, 'I know, I'll shut his hand in the door, then scare him, then get a knife and chop him into tiny little pieces!'

The next night Jim came in from doing his shopping. He opened the door and the ghost shut his hand in the door. Then the ghost scared him, then went to get the knife, but the knife just slipped out of his hands. By the time he realised his mistake Jim had run away!

Michelle Laing (11)
Collydean Primary School, Glenrothes

The Haunted House

One spooky night on Hallowe'en me and my cousin were in the house ourselves and that night we heard voices and scratches against the walls. After we heard them we decided to ignore them and get to sleep.

The next morning we went on the computer and typed in 'ghosts' and it came up famous ghosts and haunted houses, so we clicked on haunted houses and it came up with our address '271 Thistle Drive'.

When we clicked on it, it came up with where the ghosts were in the house. We clicked on that and it said that people had heard voices, people scratching their nails against the walls and calling people's names. One of the names was my cousin's name. She was not there because she wanted to stay home with her dad.

That night the ghosts came out of the wall, scared us away and took over the house. When we went back to bed, the ghosts were in the bedrooms and in the beds. We were too scared to be in the house so we went to sleep outside.

When we ran out of food and drinks we had to go back inside and get more. We couldn't go to Tesco because we didn't have any money, so we had to go inside, but we didn't want to because we didn't like getting scared by the ghosts. When we eventually went inside the ghosts weren't there and weren't ever seen again.

Stuart Callison (11)
Collydean Primary School,
Glenrothes

Moving

It was September the 11th and the Morins were moving to Old Bank Street. They arrived at exactly 2 o'clock. The two girls were watching telly and their parents were getting ready to go to a ball. The kids heard a creak so they went over to the door.

'Boo!' cried their dad and ran back to his room.

The kids silently crept to the door and ran to their mum and dad's room.

'Help you two! We need to go.'

Before their parents could say anything they shot down the stairs.

Cccccccccc. They ran upstairs to the eldest girl's room and went in. The eldest girl reached in until something pulled her in. The little girl looked away slowly not wanting to get caught. She looked around and the design on her wall had changed, it was now red and black with white ghosts all around. The ghosts on the wall were coming out but they suddenly went in.

'Hello? Mummy? Daddy?'

'She's gone!'

'Where?'

'I don't know.'

Days passed with police in and out. One day a strange painting appeared in the post. They hung it up, it was a painting of a farmhouse with their daughter in it.

Day after day the girl did not return. But every day the girl in the painting changed her position …

Lucy Metcalfe (10)
Collydean Primary School, Glenrothes

No Escape

Many years ago in Clover Avenue lived a family of four, it was a mansion they lived in.

They had servants running around for their every minute need. The mum was snobby and would not allow anything to be dirty. Jodie and Ryan were perfect, they did everything right. The father was just the same but there was one exception, he was not bothered how tidy the house was.

One morning when the wind howled round the trees and the birds were silent the two children and their mother awoke with a start. They ran to wake their father but he would not wake, he had died in his sleep. At breakfast they were not fussed about what had happened, they were too tied up in their own lives.

The servant brought them their breakfast. They sat and looked and then they drank their tea. Suddenly they all dropped dead. The servants cheered, they were free. After five minutes they were packed and ready to go but it was not that easy. The doors slammed shut and misty figures stood around the servants. 'What is this?' they screamed. 'Is this a joke because if it is it is not that funny.' The ghosts caved in on them. What was happening? The servants did not know.

'This is not a joke, this is a punishment for what you did to us,' said the ghosts.

The servants understood.

Marissa Kennedy (10)
Collydean Primary School,
Glenrothes

The Ghost Mansion

It was not long ago the Riddle family lived in this mansion. The mansion had ivy up the walls and had some windows boarded up.

Everyone thought this house was haunted because the father was hung, the boy was poisoned and the mother was stabbed the same night. The thing that worried everyone was, who was next?

One sunny day a man decided to go to the Riddle house for a visit, so he did. Everyone said it was a bad idea. He believed in himself. When he entered the mansion he saw a bright light and everything was dusty. Then he saw a white floating thing coming towards him. He fell back and banged his head. The white floating thing was a ghost named Jay, he'd seen that the man was unconscious. Jay went to get a cold bucket of water to pour over the man. The man who was named John woke up as fast as a cheetah.

'Who are you?' asked Jay.

'I-I-I'm John . . . who . . . are . . . you?'

'I'm Jay, nice to meet you.'

John decided that Jay was a friendly ghost and they started to look round and clear the house, so John could stay with him forever. Jay was so happy he began to change colours, white to yellow, yellow to orange, orange to red and back. Finally they had cleaned up and John phoned all the nervous people in town to come on up and they all lived happily ever after.

Megan Rutherford (10)
Collydean Primary School,
Glenrothes

Witchcraft

One day a three-year-old boy named George was getting his photo taken at home when suddenly he turned away and, pointing at the wall beside him, said, 'Look, old Nanny's here.'

Now this was very peculiar because his nanny had passed away just two weeks ago and no one else in the room saw anything unusual. Then their dog began barking at where George was pointing. It ran up beside George then began biting the air as if trying to catch something. The family's dog Rover never liked George's nana and always tried to bite her when he saw her. The rest of the family still didn't see anything.

When the photo was developed a strange misty shape was right next to George and Rover, exactly where they were pointing, looking, biting and barking.

The next day they visited a mystery specialist to see if it really was a ghost or something else, but the answer was, 'This photo is a genuine ghost sighting and your son will always be able to see ghosts. He will be able to communicate with them too. He is very lucky to have such a rare gift.'

As George grew up he had many ghost friends and he knew that no one else could see them. At the age of 70 he was sentenced to death on behalf of witchcraft. On the 5th of November he was burnt in the middle of town.

Katherine Horsburgh (10)
Collydean Primary School,
Glenrothes

A Walk To A Graveyard

It was a beautiful, sunny, autumn morning. The birds were singing and the squirrels were gathering nuts for the winter. I called Jodie on my mobile to see if she would like to go to the park.

'Yes of course I'd like to,' she said. 'Come down in five minutes.'

So I went to ask Mum and she said yes.

When we got to the park we found a secret passageway through the woods. Jodie just ran ahead through the wood so I had to follow her. We went on for a while and then just as I was about to collapse we saw a big black house. We went up a narrow path and into a graveyard. It was really creepy. All the gravestones were covered in moss and had fallen down. The grass was overgrown and there were big bats flying about. I went first, Jodie close behind me and then, we froze.

In front of us was a ghost, pulling all of the moss off the graves. I looked up. Jodie screamed and we backed off. It was wearing the strangest clothes. A leather jacket with a skull on fire, a chain round its neck and it had spiky ghost hair. He came up to us and screamed. We screamed as well and ran away. We looked back but there was no sign of him chasing us so we got home safely.

Stephanie Arnott (10)
Collydean Primary School, Glenrothes

Time Traveller

One night I was walking to a farm in Pitcairn early in the morning. It was exactly 2am. I started at 3am. I milked the cows, fed the sheep, prepared the horses and fed the hens. I walked into a strange tree. I looked up and saw a rusty, engraved gold key.

I reached up and I pulled. I spun round and round and suddenly I got chucked out. I landed in a haystack; a horse was sleeping beside it. I woke it up and put a saddle, bridle and reins on it.

I rode it to a castle. I opened the door. It was beautifully decorated. The stairs were gold with a red carpet. The banister was gold. The walls were gold with portraits of Mary Queen of Scots, her family and Lord Darnly.

I walked up the stairs and saw a chambermaid coming from a room. The chambermaid didn't see me because I'd travelled back in time. I went into the room and saw Mary Queen of Scots sleeping. A fire was burning softly. There was a dressing table with a beautiful golden mirror.

I went to the landing and walked downstairs and out the door, there was the royal tennis courts and the most beautiful garden in the world. I went to the orchard and there it was - a big, creepy, floating, grey ghost of a bull with a big, sharp pair of horns.

The bull chased me to the top of Falkland Hill then I let go of the key and reappeared at the farm.

Niall Haughey (10)
Collydean Primary School,
Glenrothes

The Ghost Of The Woods

About 4 years ago there were 2 girls camping in the woods. They were called Heather and Chloe. They had been waiting for this day for weeks! They'd taken one big tent with them because in some ways they were scared but in others they were excited. They had also taken food for a midnight feast. Food like crisps, sweets and chocolate. They thought it would be one of the best days of their lives, but that was not true.

They left the house at 3pm. They were planning to stay in the woods until 12pm the next day.

It was after 1am. Their parents were worried about them. So they went into the woods that Heather and Chloe went to. But they were not there. Hours passed by, their mother and father started to cry. It was now 5.30. They phoned the police because that was all they had left to do.

Their father saw something in the far distance, he thought it was a ghost! Even though he was scared he did not tell anyone because they would think that he was lying.

Finally the police arrived. Again hours passed by. They started to cry. They were starting to think that they were dead!

The police sadly said, 'We have to give up.'

They cried again.

Their father said, 'We will come back tomorrow.'

So they went home.

A ghost's voice said, 'I killed them . . .'

Emily Reid (10)
Collydean Primary School,
Glenrothes

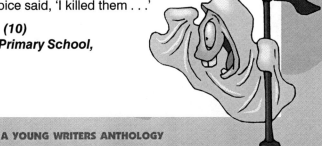

The Farmer's Ghost

'Nooo!' I woke up in Emily's bedroom. I was shaking all over. Sweat was pouring down my face. I peered over to Emily's clock. It was 2.05am. Suddenly Bella, Emily's dog gave a loud bark and Emily sat bolt upright.

'What was that?' she said in a shaky voice.

'I don't know,' I said, 'let's go see.'

So we grabbed Emily's plastic golf clubs and slowly began to walk down the stairs. We went into Emily's sister Miriam's bedroom. She was sitting up in bed.

'We need you to search the house with us,' we said. So off we went.

We entered the living room and a terrifying sight met our eyes. There, in the middle of the room, was the ghost of a farmer. He pointed a bony finger at us.

'This house has been built over my farm,' he said in a spooky voice. 'You shall pay!'

We ran out of the house but the ghost followed us. We ran into the woods and there, in front of us, was a gravestone. It said 'Ben Foe - he loved this place'. I grabbed a stone and threw it hard at the grave.

Suddenly it began to glow an illuminous green. The ghost began to be sucked back into the grave. 'You will pay!' he screamed.

There was total silence. We began to walk towards Emily's house. We walked into the living room and sat down on the sofa. We agreed to never mention it again.

Jasmine Stenhouse (10)
Collydean Primary School, Glenrothes

The Haunted Amusement Park

I was walking through an abandoned amusement park at night. It was foggy and dark. I could feel the damp, gritty ground underneath the soles of my white Nike trainers. It was Friday 13th.

In the distance I could see the haunted house. Suddenly a clear image with red eyes came through the door, it turned and saw me. It started to chase me, I ran and ran and soon came to the tall, silver helter-skelter that glistened in the moonlight.

I turned the door handle but it did not open. I rammed it again and it burst open like a bottle of wine. I rushed in, and locked the door with the key I'd found on the floor. The ghost flew through the tall, old wooden door and chased me out again, this time I decided to go into the green glass maze, a maze that is full of green glass mirrors. I crossed the gritty ground to the glass mirrors.

As I ran through the maze, there were about 5 of me. I came to a dead end. I was panting for breath. Soon I fell to the green ground exhausted and the ghost came. My eyes shut as the devil ghost and the rest of them came through me, they took my spirit …

I had become a ghost enclosed in the haunted amusement park.

The next year my little sister came into the amusement park but she was killed by the ghosts

I faced. As I saw the ghosts eat her up, it was then that I opened up my eyes and found myself lying in my wooden bed facing the ceiling. When I went up for breakfast my sister was nowhere to be seen . . .

Claire Pollock (10)
Collydean Primary School, Glenrothes

The Small Cottage

On top of a hill lay a small cottage that was said to be haunted. A little girl was delivering cookies. The last delivery was the cottage. She didn't think anything of it and went climbing up the hill.

At the top of the hill stood a dog-like figure. When she was up there she pressed the bell and saw a white dog come through the door. The girl got the shock of her life and ran to the side of the gate and tripped over a stone.

She woke up about 10 minutes later and saw a little boy ghost staring over her with his dog licking her face.

'Hi,' said the girl, pushing the dog away and standing up at the same time.

'Hi, my name's Tammy, would you like to buy some cookies?'

'No thanks, we've just had our dinner, but would you like to play?'

'OK, but only for a little while.'

After 40 minutes of playing on the trampoline, swing and in the pond Tammy thought it was time to go, but before she'd asked him what his name was he just said, 'You'll never know.'

Tammy kept going to see him but 6 days had past since playing with him. She went all the way up the hill and didn't see any cottage. Tammy sat down and started crying. Suddenly she saw a foggy cloud with his face in. He said, 'Kyle' quite loudly. Suddenly she realised that was his name and started smiling again.

Karianne Stenhouse (11)
Collydean Primary School, Glenrothes

Scary Ghost

I was walking to my gran's house. I went in the door, there was nobody there so I went upstairs, nobody there either.

I went to watch the telly so I turned the switch on, then I put the telly on but it didn't come on, as somebody had turned it off.

Then I saw a ghost, it was scary so I ran out of the door. 'Boo!' It was there too, I quickly grabbed the phone to call the police then the answer machine came on so I went in the cupboard.

The door opened, it was my gran. I told her that I'd seen a ghost, she didn't believe me, she thought I was lying but I wasn't. I saw it again so did my gran.

It was talking. It said, 'Come out wherever you are!'

We phoned the police again, we told the police there was a ghost in the house.

The police took 10 minutes to arrive. 'Where did you see the ghost?'

'Behind the telly!'

So they checked.

'Boo!'

The police screamed, 'Argh!'

It flew out of the house and said, 'I'll be back for you!'

The next day we saw the ghost again so we tried to fight it - my gran hit it with a frying pan, I squirted ketchup at it too! We got a box and we tried to catch it, we missed it the first and second time but then we caught it - third time lucky!

Ian Balfour (11)
Collydean Primary School, Glenrothes

Ghost Pie

One dark, dull night an old ghost sat in his armchair. He lived on his own (with a few spiders and rats) in the huge mansion he owned. Nobody liked him as they thought he was mean.

Suddenly there was a knock on the wooden door. No one had knocked on it for years.

The door creaked as he opened the door. Standing there was a fluffy bunny with evil green eyes.

'Hi, I'm Henry,' it said sweetly, 'would you like some strawberry pies?' it offered.

'How much?' the old ghost said gruffly.

'Free!' it replied, handing him 5 strawberry pies and hopped away.

The old ghost shut the door and waddled off to his chair. The sweet smell of strawberries went up his nose. The strawberry sauce dripped down his chin. One after the other a pie went into his mouth.

After a few minutes they were gone. 'Yum-yum,' he said, patting his stomach. He walked up the stairs to bed. When he reached it, he climbed in and curled up tightly.

At about 1 o'clock his stomach started rumbling. He climbed out of bed and went to the toilet. As he sat on the seat his stomach started roaring. The toilet vibrated, his ectoplast stretched and then he

exploded. All that was left were his glasses on the floor …
Scurrying along the ground was a small, brown mouse.

After a while the house was sold and Henry and the old
ghost (mouse) were never seen again.

Michelle Proudfoot (11)
Collydean Primary School, Glenrothes

Ghost Alert

One dark, stormy night a 19-year-old girl moved into a haunted mansion. She did not know that it was haunted though. The girl's name was Kimmy. Hundreds of years ago there had lived a horrible, nasty, terrifying man. He lived in the very same mansion. It had been said that the man had been stabbed in the heart by a bodybuilder. The man turned into a ghost. It was also said that he had glow-in-the-dark, extremely sharp teeth.

'If you go in you will never come out again,' said one of her friends, the day before.

When she had moved in she felt quite excited but scared at the same time. She was scared in case the rumours were true. There were 20 bedrooms. Kimmy picked the room closest to the front door. That night she unpacked and could not get to sleep until about 2 o'clock.

None of her friends came because they were too chicken to go. After a couple of weeks Kimmy had settled in fully. On the Friday it was the 13th. At night she was just about to go to bed and Kimmy saw nothing but extremely sharp glow-in-the-dark teeth. It was the ghost!

All of a sudden the door slammed shut and *'Boo!'* Kimmy Text was never seen again!

Shannon Blackwood (11)
Collydean Primary School,
Glenrothes

The Haunted Graveyard

One night at midnight Joanna came to see her grandma's grave. It looked like no one had been there for years and years. There were cobwebs everywhere. She was sweating with fear, so she quickly put some flowers down and she tried to run away but there was a shadow moving.

She was shaking, her whole body was shaking. She was surrounded by shadows. She was shouting for help, she shouted millions of times but no one heard her.

Joanna kept really still then the shadows just vanished in the blink of an eye. So she ran away and only went back to the grave with her mum and dad.

Jennifer Davies (8)
Drighlington Primary School, Bradford

Crawler Hive

It was a dark and gloomy night. Paul stood in the graveyard waiting for Luke. A howl came from the deep grass. 'What the heck was that?' he asked himself. Suddenly a man came running with blood gushing out from his neck.

'Werewolf!' the man screamed.

'Where?' Paul asked.

'In Crawler Hive,' the man replied.

'What's all the commotion?' Luke asked as he ran into the graveyard.

'In Crawler Hive there is a werewolf. Do you want to go in?'

'Yes,' Luke replied.

As they stumbled in another howl came from deep within …

Michael Smithson (8)
Drighlington Primary School, Bradford

The Invisible Path

It was a misty and stormy night when a clap of thunder woke a child. He could not get back to sleep so he went to the living room when another clap of thunder highlighted a beastly face pressed against the window.

'Argh!' he screamed.

His parents made no sound. He went to investigate.

It was 2 o'clock in the morning and the boy was following adult-sized footprints. It led to a path he had never seen in daylight. He followed. It went to a cave. He went inside.

'The way is shut. It was made by those who are dead, and the dead keep it,' said an eerie voice.

Then out of nowhere a scabbed ghost appeared. 'You entered our domain, now you must die,' it said.

A ghost city appeared and loads more ghosts too.

'The way is shut. It was made by those who are dead and the dead keep it,' said the ghosts. Then the boy died with fright.

Even now, 5 years later, the howls of the boy still echo from the cave.

Cain Harniess (8)
Drighlington Primary School, Bradford

The Shadow

One misty night Jack was taking the bins out when, out of the corner of his eye, he saw a dark shadow. He ran in the opposite direction but it was there again. He ran and ran but it was following him. It followed him to the old house in the wood.

He ran to the door and ran inside, up the creaky steps and into the study. The shadow couldn't get him. *Thump! Thump!* The shadow was banging on the door. The door flew off the frame. Then he could see it was the ghost of his father.

His father came up to him and told him he had to go up to Heaven with him. He was the chosen one. He had to go or else the whole world would die out. Then the ghost vanished.

He was starting to go white and float up and up and no one saw him again.

Jack Bentley (9)
Drighlington Primary School, Bradford

The Spooky Forest

One mysterious night it was all quiet and misty when I was on a walk through the forest and back to my house. I crossed the road and it was a little bit scary when I got in.

I heard this noise running across the bushes but I kept on walking on, then I saw a creepy thing staring right at me with bloody eyes. I heard a car coming so I went back, I saw it was Calum and Luke.

Liam said, 'Thank God you guys are here, there is some weird things going on around here. Keep a good look out!'

We kept on walking down to the forest, when we heard a weird noise like bones dropping from a skeleton. We looked and we saw a werewolf; it howled.

We all shouted, 'Werewolf!'

We ran through the forest and spotted another werewolf so we ran even faster. We got back just in time for dinner. We felt really scared and petrified when we got home and the werewolves were still out there …

Liam Bailey (8)
Drighlington Primary School, Bradford

Haunted Castle

A week before Hallowe'en Annie and I needed to go on a vacation to a place called Haunted Island to investigate the weird goings on. Before we knew it, it was Thursday, the day that we were going.

In the airport we got something to eat and we were waiting for the lady to say, 'Passengers for Haunted Island please come to gate 38'. Annie and I were bored on the plane then finally we saw Haunted Island. Annie and I went to a hotel where we got unpacked and settled in.

'So, what are we doing here anyway?' Annie said.

'We're here to see what's so weird about this place,' I said.

Annie and I looked around the place. We went down to the restaurant in the hotel and asked the lady, 'What's so weird about this place?' but she didn't say anything.

On Friday it was Hallowe'en. Annie and I went guising and we went up to the castle that people were warning us not to go to, but we went anyway.

We heard someone screaming. Annie and I went into the castle. We needed to split up, I went one way, she went the other. I bumped into a vampire, it almost bit me. Annie walked right through a ghost. The vampire vanished.

On the way Annie and I found some clues. These clues led up to a bat. The bat was on the ceiling but I wasn't scared.

Annie and I heard people singing in the castle, so we went to see what was going on. Annie and I joined in so we could get some clues and we did.

A little while later, we found out that a guy called Zombos was trying to take over the world. We called the police and they came and took him to jail.

Kristina Bassett (10)
Dunblane Primary School, Dunblane

A Spooky Graveyard

One dark and stormy night when the crashes of thunder shook your bones a young girl called Nicola was watching TV.

Her parents said, 'We're off out for a walk.'

They were quickly out of the door, she tried to follow them but they were too fast and she went the wrong way. That way led to a graveyard.

When she looked in the church she saw a shadow in the shape of a witch. She turned around in shock and when she turned back around there was a bony hand sticking out of every grave. She ran out of the graveyard and into the woods which led back to her house …

Sarah Cowles (8)
Drighlington Primary School, Bradford

Hallowe'en

I woke up on Hallowe'en, I went downstairs and it started to chuck it down with rain. There was a lot of thunder and lightning. I made some toast and *zap* I started to travel back in time.

Pop! I was in a castle, it was Stirling Castle. *Pop! Pop!* Suddenly a load of ghosts and ghouls.

At that same moment Jonathan, Micah, Stewart, Douglas, Ian, William, Calum and Ewan ran in.

'Alex get out of there,' said Ian.

But it was too late all the ghosts and ghouls surrounded us.

We ran straight through the ghosts.

Death shouted, 'Stop!' when we got to the dungeon …

Alex Glass (10)
Dunblane Primary School, Dunblane

The Night Of The Castle Fright!

One Hallowe'en night in a castle in Scotland, Dracula was pacing up and down in front of Frankenstein muttering to himself. 'How am I going to get rid of that brother of Calum Spooner's? He almost killed me!' said Dracula.

'How about,' said Frankenstein, 'we kidnap Calum and Ewan will come and find him so we can kill him.'

'Brilliant,' shouted Dracula. 'Gather my army, bring me ghosts and my Grim Reaper, my headless horseman, my headless warrior and my evil witches,' he cried.

Two days later Dracula had his army ready.

'Let's go,' yelled Dracula.

Two hours later they arrived and Calum was bound and gagged and pulled up into Dracula's plane and off they went. When Calum woke up he had no idea where he was, he tried to speak but the gag was over his mouth.

Next morning when Ewan woke up he called, 'Come on Calum there's school today.' There was no answer. 'That's strange,' said Ewan, 'I'll go and find him.'

As he went downstairs he saw Dracula and Frankenstein's initials on the wall, *Dracula,* thought Ewan and off he went to Dracula's castle.

When he got to Dracula's castle he slipped in by the window and fell onto Calum. 'Calum,' said Ewan. He untied Calum and stood up.

As they went to the door Dracula appeared in front of them! Suddenly white sparks flashed out of Dracula's eyes. Ewan fell to the ground.

'Nooooo!' cried Calum and rushed at Dracula, Dracula flew backwards, hit the wall and lay unconscious on the ground. Calum picked up Ewan and ran out of the castle and into the woods, then Ewan woke up.

'Good,' said Calum.

'Let's go home,' said Ewan.

So off they went.

Calum Spooner (10)
Dunblane Primary School, Dunblane

A Spooktacular Hallowe'en!

I was going to the Hallowe'en disco as a cowgirl. Natalie was going as Dracula, Kayleigh was a vampire bat and Rachel was a witch. Natalie and Kayleigh went to the toilet while Rachel and I danced for about half an hour. Kayleigh and Natalie weren't back.

'We'd better see if they're OK,' I shouted over the music.

Me and Rachel went up to the toilets.

'Oh no!' gasped Rachel.

I nearly fainted, 'It's Dracula, Frankenstein, Bloody Baron and Headless Horseman! Where's Kayleigh and Natalie?' I exclaimed.

'In there!' Dracula pointed to the boys' toilets.

'What!' cried Rachel.

We both ran into the boys' toilets. Dracula grabbed us. I got the water gun and soaked him.

We rescued Kayleigh and Natalie. That was one spooktacular Hallowe'en.

Jill Hinchliffe (10)
Dunblane Primary School, Dunblane

The Siege Of Blood Castle

The dark light of Blood Castle is a cold feeling. It makes me and my friends shiver with fear but the fear of the ghost warriors spooks me.

The campground is in a small ditch about 30 yards off from Blood Castle and we can hear the endless screams of the prisoners. Why are we in this ditch? We are waiting for Frankenstein's knights. We are waiting for the knights so we can throw stones at them and knock them off their horses so we can lay siege to the castle. Success in our campaign looks sure to be marked by the privation of many lives.

'I think we should attack now!' shouts Douglas.

'No, no, no!' I shout in reply.

'Speaking of knights, here they come!' Ewan says in shock.

The Frankenstein knights go by when I shout, 'Attack!'

We win the battle and me and my friends march towards Blood Castle to kill the Grim Reaper king …

Neil Alexander (10)
Dunblane Primary School, Dunblane

Hallowe'en Surprises

Once upon a Hallowe'en, when Jenny the fake witch and Katy the wicked queen were guising the horrific haunted street called Mulberry Drive (cheery name, not the place) in Transylvania, at 9pm, they were terrified and alone. Jenny, a very wild brunette with a jolly smile, was a 'spooktacular' witch and Katy, a very laid-back character with extremely long hair, was a petrifying queen. After a while Helen and Melody their arch-enemies, appeared. A nasty couple with sly expressions and beady eyes. Helen wore a costume of a headless girl and Melody was a spooky ghost.

There was a trail of chicken feed on the ground, so the girls followed it. Melody and Helen starting slagging Jenny and Katy off and boasting. 'We'll get more sweets than you, ha-ha!' Helen chanted.

Katy added, 'Bet the chicken'll get you.'

They knocked on the door of a castle, believed to be Dracula's. The door swung open and they stepped inside. There was a blinding flash and all Jenny and Katy could see was Melody and Helen being executed at the top of the stairs and blood seeping through everything.

'We'll be next!' Katy squealed.

'Escape!' Jenny wailed but they couldn't. The door was sealed. It was a Hallowe'en trap.

'If you don't want to be murdered, kill the mad chicken. If you succeed you go home. If you don't, the chicken eats you,' Dracula thundered. But Jenny and Katy had already slain the mad chicken. *Poof!* They were back home.

'Never again,' they said together.

Christie Mackie (9)
Dunblane Primary School, Dunblane

A Spooky Hallowe'en

It was the evening before Hallowe'en. Me, Charlotte, Holly and Catherine were riding up to Sorcerer's Castle. It was a long ride and very dark. By the time we got there it was midnight. We put our horses in the stables and nervously approached the door into the castle. I knocked once and the door creaked open. We stepped inside …

Bang! The door slammed shut.

'Well let's find our room,' said Holly nervously.

We walked up and up until we found a room.

'I'll have this bed,' I said.

'I'll have this one!' said Charlotte.

'I'll have this one!' said Holly.

'And I'll have this one!' said Catherine.

At midnight . . .

Bonggg! The clock struck twelve.

'Whooo!' a voice howled.

The voice came closer.

'Whooooo,' it got louder.

I woke up and startled by the noise I looked up.

'Aarrgghh!' I screamed.

Everyone else woke up.

'Aarrgghh!' we all screamed.

In front of us was a ghost with no head and one leg!

We grabbed our stuff and ran outside. We got on our horses and rode out of the place.

'That's the last time I go there!' I said.

We all agreed.

Rosalind Wildman (9)
Dunblane Primary School, Dunblane

All Hallows Eve

As the train rumbled to a stop I was greeted by a grumpy-looking driver, Auntie Bass and a hyper-looking Craig. They took me into their Mini and we went trundling off …

When we arrived at Kreecran I saw the colossal castle I would be staying in for the next several days. Then finally I opened the door and went in.

I was greeted by Edward the doorman, followed by Adan and the not-so-friendly Kay. Then a servant came and took my coat and luggage and showed me to my room.

That night I kept hearing a screaming and at midnight the clock struck thirteen! I decided to take a look …

I woke Adan and we decided to take a look and we saw a moaning, grief-stricken, middle-aged woman screaming, a dead man sprawled over her arms. Tears were streaking down her face. I had to leave the scene.

Adan and I thought about it over the next few days and finally on the last morning I asked Auntie Bass if this place was haunted. She said that her grandmother had been visited by a murderer one night. Her husband had tried to protect her but she was killed, so whenever there's a visitor she haunts. *Sussed!*

Micah Nye (10)
Dunblane Primary School,
Dunblane

Spooky Hallowe'en!

It was Hallowe'en and there was a disco at Stirling Castle, Jill and I went to the toilet, we went in and suddenly the door locked, Jill *screamed!*

'Shh!' I said.

But then a voice shouted, 'Hello girls.'

The boys and Max heard Jill scream and they came to unlock the door. After five whole hours they finally got it open.

Everyone went behind the curtains on the stage. Suddenly something that looked like Frankenstein came and jumped out at us.

We screamed and all his friends came, we ran like rockets. He got us.

We screamed and shouted but he didn't let go. They locked us in the cellar. We kept banging and shouting.

Then suddenly Frankenstein stumbled as he was walking in we didn't. We didn't stop screaming then Max found a door and we escaped and never went to the castle again.

Rachel Craig (10)
Dunblane Primary School, Dunblane

The Horror Goes On

A long time ago there were four girls, Lauren, Tasha, Natalie and Kayleigh. They were all going guising near a big castle. Lauren was a cat, Tasha was a witch, Kayleigh was a bat and Natalie was a vampire. They knocked on the big castle door and it opened by itself. They all shivered as they all went into the castle … 'Argh!' *Whoosh,* down they fell through a trapdoor.

'Hello my pretties,' croaked a voice.

'What was that?' said Kayleigh.

'It sounded like an old granny,' said Tasha.

'I'm glad I'm having you for dinner!' came the voice again.

'If you're not a granny then what are you?'

'I'm glad you asked. I'm a witch, ha, ha, ha!'

'Yes I'm very glad as well and, oh, I'm a vampire!' came a voice from nowhere.

'This is the worst Hallowe'en ever,' moaned Lauren.

'Yes it is if we're going to be eaten!' said Natalie.

'Oh let me go home!' said Tasha, then she fell over and the wall opened.

'Hey now we can escape!'

The vampire swooped and shut the door so that no one could escape.

We escaped anyway and left the witch and vampire to fight each other … and we never went back to that castle!

Natalie Turnbull (10)
Dunblane Primary School, Dunblane

The Haunted Mansion

On the 31st of October 2013 at midnight some strange things happened.

'Help,' cried Calum.

'Save him!' shouted Ewan. 'Get him down.'

'Hhhaaa,' cackled the witch. Then she disappeared into thin air.

'He's gone and it's school tomorrow,' whispered Shaun.

'We've got to save him,' screamed Susan.

Broom, broom.

'Hey what's that?' asked Paul.

'Hey, want a ride to get away from those headless warriors? Quick,' said Ewan.

Clank, clank went the armour of the warriors. *Clank, clank.*

'Welcome,' laughed a voice. It was Dracula!

'Help!' screamed Ellen and Caitlin.

'Run kids,' said Fiona.

'Yeah, run,' said Alistair.

'Never,' cried Skeleton, 'never!'

'Yeah we will,' laughed Ewan. *Kaboom* went some thunder exploding, from the sky it appeared.

Suddenly I saw a sign saying *The Haunted Mansion, Beware Whoever Comes In Never Comes Out!*

'Argh,' screamed Ellen and fell to the ground and died. I was just in time to see the headless warriors cut her head off.

'Ow, that looks sore,' sniffed Caitlin.

'You're next girl,' shouted Dracula.

'Um, um,' muffled a voice, 'um, um.' It was Calum wearing a gag.

'Ho, ho,' laughed Ewan, 'are you all right Calum?'

Ewan took the gag off. Then a laugh exploded out of the sky.

'Ha, ha, ha.' It was a witch. 'Death acus,' spat the witch.

The purplish spell hit Calum.

'Right,' said Ewan, 'time to go home.'

Ewan Couper (10)
Dunblane Primary School, Dunblane

Hallowe'en

'Jonathan you have got to go and get your friends to come and visit the cave.'

Ten minutes later everyone arrived. We walked over to the cave and to our surprise Spectre appeared and zapped us back to the house and straight into the television set.

'Where are we?' whispered Douglas.

'It looks like we are trapped inside a horror movie,' replied Alex.

'Eek!' screamed Jonathan as he started to run.

'Why are you running?' asked Stewart.

'Ghosts behind you.'

Everyone turned, saw the ghosts and ran but we ran into a graveyard and the zombies came out of the graves. Then bats came one way so we ran towards the castle, it was the only way left. We ran into the castle and stopped just in time because there was a trapdoor. We grabbed a loose floorboard and pulled and eventually we got out but the ghosts, zombies and the bats caught up with us and chased us to a place that had swinging axes. We ran judging out timing very carefully because one hit from an axe would chop you in half.

Eventually we got past them all, it was a dead end. One of the zombies pushed us and we hit a brick that was sticking out and the wall spun round. Now it was a real dead end, nothing except 3 walls, a ceiling and ghosts, bats and zombies. They came closer and closer.

'Jonathan wake up.'

Jonathan Hodgson (10)
Dunblane Primary School, Dunblane

The Mysterious Madman

She came out of the gas station with a packet of wine gums. It was raining heavily in the dark as she walked home. The road was quiet and deserted. Her day hadn't gone as she had planned. All she needed now was more stress. Suddenly out of nowhere a long black car stopped. A tall man in black got out. She couldn't quite make out his face because his old tatty hat was in the way. Minding her own business she carried on walking. The man slowly started to walk towards her. However there was something about those footsteps, they didn't sound right. They weren't normal, and she noticed it. She now was starting to feel uncomfortable. It was like she was being followed.

She walked quickly, eager to get home as soon as possible. She didn't even dare to look back to see if he had gone. Whoever he was he was mad. 'If this is a dream then I want to wake up right now,' she mumbled.

She was breathing heavily. With the keys ready in her hand she opened the door. She ran inside slamming the door shut behind her, she peeped out the window. He had disappeared to her relief. She went to the kitchen and helped herself to a glass of champagne. Controlling her unsteady hand she took a sip. *Crack!* She let go of her glass. Outside the garden window she could see him.

'Oh no,' she screamed, 'just leave me alone.'

There he was in the middle of the garden holding a huge, metre-long axe.

He started to break the garden door. Panicking she immediately ran up the stairs. Quickly making up her mind she hid in the wardrobe. As she leant back she felt something soft. It was a great shock to find her brother's dead body. She was feeling sick so she hid under the bed. Dialling 999, she tried to call the police, but the lines were dead

… slowly she turned her head around. Sitting next to her was the madman trying to slaughter her. She could feel the hairs curl up her spine. So she leapt from under the bed, to the outside of her house.

Unexpectedly someone tapped her shoulder, it was the mysterious madman. 'Happy Hallowe'en Jane.'

'David, I thought you …'

'Oh that, that was hours ago.' And with that he took Jane back inside the house with a nasty grin on his face …

Nisha Singadia (11)
Hall Green Secondary School, Birmingham

The Dog

There was a girl called Molly, her great-grandmother had just died and she had passed down her old cottage to Molly, but until Molly visited the cottage she didn't realise her grandmother had a dog. The dog was a golden retriever called Sundance and it was quite old but enjoyed Molly's company.

It was a Friday night when Molly spent the night at the cottage and it was bitterly cold, but Molly and Sundance sat by the huge log fire. It was past 10 o'clock when Molly finally went to bed and Sundance jumped on the bed with her.

Molly was just at the stage where she was drifting off to sleep when she heard a dripping sound. Molly got out of bed to investigate the noise. The dripping sound was coming from the bathroom, from the old rusty tap. She turned the tap off and went back to bed. Before Molly went to sleep, she felt under the bed for Sundance who had crept under there when she was in the bathroom and he licked her hand.

Later, Molly heard the dripping sound again and felt under the bed for Sundance but the dog was not there. Molly suddenly heard a loud bark …

A long, bony hand clasped the door and yanked it off its hinges, Molly screamed, she didn't know what it was, but all she knew was it was going to get her. Molly grabbed a baseball bat and edged her way across the wall closer and closer to the menacing creature. She bravely peeped behind the door.

The creature was bending over Sundance sinking its sharp fangs into the dog's scruffy neck. Molly suddenly sneezed loudly and the creature flipped round, hissed loudly at Molly, blood dripping from its fangs and flew through the French windows shattering them completely.

A few years later Molly (who was now 29) had married a man called Paul (who was a plumber and was also 29). They both had a son called Dale and lived very happily. The old cottage had been turned into a plumbing centre and Molly worked there answering calls. Sundance, the now very old dog, lived with Paul and Molly playing with Dale all the time.

One night Molly was working a late shift all by herself in the dark waiting for a call. She was reading 'Hello' magazine chuckling at the naked photos of Shane Ritchie at a London nightclub.

Molly started thinking about the time when the creature came to the cottage, it sent a massive shiver up her spine. Suddenly a bang came from the store room, Molly went to investigate. She opened the door and in a flash the same creature made its way towards her, its big, gaping jaws ready to clasp her neck. It was then that Molly realised that the monster was a Jabberwocky, a creature of the night, a menacing monster making terror, it stamped to her in a half revengeful, half delighted way.

Later on at about 12.09 Paul came to pick Molly up. When he came in it was the last thing he saw ...

Georgie Bonnell (11)
Hall Green Secondary School,
Birmingham

The Tall, Dark Stranger

'Come on,' said Claire, nagging to the others that were puffing and panting behind. It was a dark and rainy night at the graveyard. All the trees were swaying in the wind. They finally got to the spot they were looking for. It was all mouldy on the grave and it looked as though the mould had been there for years. It was one of their grandads who had died in the war. Suddenly there was a rustling in the trees.

'What's that noise?' said Sam, looking worried.

'There wasn't a noise and don't be daft,' replied Lydia.

They all heard the noise this time.

'Told you,' whispered Sam.

'*Run*!' shouted Claire, with the man behind following every step they took!

They were all running as fast as they could to get out of the graveyard, but could hardly see in front of them as the rain was lashing down and getting in their eyes. Lydia noticed the door was open to the church so she quietly said, 'Let's go and hide in the church and wait for the man to go.'

They all crept in to find a place to hide.

Sam said, 'Here is a door which leads up to the bell tower, shall we go up there?'

Just as they were going to go up the stairs they heard the cobbled stones outside the church door making a crunching noise.

They immediately rushed behind the curtain which was at the top of the altar and made no sound at all.

The church door creaked open and the girls saw a silhouette figure of a tall man wearing a long coat standing there breathing heavily. The man began to walk into the church, he kept stopping and looking round. The girls got more and more anxious, their hearts were beating faster and faster. The strange man was getting closer and closer …

All of a sudden Claire realised that her foot was showing from beneath the curtain. She immediately pulled back her foot. The strange man noticed the curtains moving. He came nearer and nearer to the girls. The girls could nearly see his face.

'What are we going to do now?' said Claire quietly.

Lydia replied, 'Shall we just try and make a run for it out of the church?'

They all said, 'Yes.'

Unfortunately for them it was too late. The strange man pulled back the curtains, the girls screamed, which echoed around the empty church, but they soon realised it was the face of Lydia's dad. Her dad had originally tried to play a trick on them but it did not work out this time!

Claire Norris (11)
Hall Green Secondary School, Birmingham

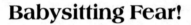

Babysitting Fear!

Georgie was walking to her best friend Molly's house. Molly lived next door to a graveyard. It was midnight. Georgie looked up and all that she could see was the moon glowing in the darkness.

Georgie finally reached Molly's house. She knocked on the door, Molly opened it.

'Hi Georgie I will be back in about three hours.'

Georgie went to Molly's house to babysit her two children Nisha and Charlotte. Molly slammed the door shut and went. Georgie went into the living room and sat down on the bright pink sofa. Suddenly she saw a faint shadow of a person. Georgie screamed!

All Georgie could hear was the tap dripping, *drip, drip*. Georgie tried to keep as still as a statue. The person standing in front of Georgie looked weird, Georgie could see through the shadow. Georgie screamed, 'Help!' but nobody heard her, it felt like she didn't exist anymore. 'If this is a dream then wake up please,' Georgie mumbled quietly to herself. But now she knew she was not in a dream, this was real. She froze with shock. 'Please don't hurt me.' But the person walked up to Georgie and touched her shoulder. 'Bring it on,' she said in her head but somehow the person heard her and took out a sparkling sharp knife. The person waved it in front of Georgie's face. She gasped.

'Go away, what have I ever done to you?' Georgie knew it was a ghost.

She tried to run away but the ghost held her back. She felt like she had Superglue on her bottom. But when the ghost was not looking she ran up to the kitchen door but it was locked. All she could do now was hope that the ghost wouldn't kill her. She was trapped, there was no way out. She screamed again at the top of her voice, but still nobody heard her.

Georgie had just thought of a way out of the mess. She ran as fast as she could through the ghost and then headed to the front door. The ghost was floating in mid-air and grabbed her neck, Georgie could not breathe. Her face turned bright purple, the ghost thought she was going to explode but it wouldn't let go.

'This might be the day that you die,' the ghost said, as if this was a joke.

The ghost let go of Georgie's neck and floated back. Then he came and stabbed Georgie in the stomach and she had a big hole in her. Blood was pouring everywhere and the pink carpet turned bright red. Georgie fell on the floor. Nisha and Charlotte ran downstairs and saw Georgie. They could see right through her. Had Georgie turned into a ghost … ?

Zarah Ahmed (11)
Hall Green Secondary School, Birmingham

A Short Horror Story

It was a dark November night. The silence as deadly as a cobra's venom, only to be broken by a shrill scream that sent a shiver up my spine. It sent an alarming message to my brain, *fear*! Something evil was lurking in the shadows of my own house. I did not know where. There was something distinct about this particular night. It felt strange and extraordinary. But I couldn't figure out why.

I had just returned from Blockbusters with a film that was the most scary horror film ever made - or so I was told. It was called 'The Ring'. It was rated a five star horror film. I thought I would give it a try. I hoped that this was a proper horror film. The last one I saw was a flop. I watched it in the cinema, but ended up walking out halfway through it. I wanted this horror film to be scary, so scary that I'd have to sleep with the light on for a month.

Anyway, I was just about to take my seat when I heard another scream, this one more ear-piercing than the first. It sounded like nothing I'd ever heard before.

Finally I managed to sit down to watch the film. I pressed play. Nothing happened, the screen was black so I pressed fast forward. Still nothing happened. Suddenly I felt scared. I was alone on this spine-chilling night. Just that second I heard the theme tune from 'The Exorcist'. An orange and red ring of fire appeared on the television screen. I could now make out weird noises in the background. Noises that I'd never heard before.

It then came to me; this was just the trailer to the film. When the film started it was about a girl called Mina

Harker who lived on an old farm that had been out of action for many years. Nothing ever changed on this farm since her great grandparents had been alive.

She was watching a film that a friend had lent her. Barely a moment after the film had finished the phone rang loudly. She picked it up and put the phone to her ear, only to hear a gruff, low-pitched voice croak, 'You're going to die seven days from today, exactly.'

The film ended that moment. I thought to myself, *this must be the worst film I'd ever seen. Even worse than the one I watched in the cinema the other day.*

The high-pitched ring of the telephone disturbed the quiet atmosphere. I picked it up. To my astonishment I heard a familiar voice croak, 'You're going to die seven days from today, exactly.'

I dropped the phone as fear invaded my body. My entire body was numb. After hesitation I grasped the phone from the floor and dialled 100 for the operator.

'Can I help you?' said the polite voice of the operator.

I replied, 'I wonder if you could trace a number for me, as I have been receiving peculiar phone calls.'

The operator agreed and promised to ring back with the information as soon as possible.

In approximately five minutes the operator rang back with the number of the last caller, I couldn't thank him enough. Straight away I punched the number in the address book of my phone. It appeared on my phone 'Lewis mobile'. I should have known better. I had met him earlier that day in Blockbusters. He must have known that I'd hired this film.

Vikash Chavda (15)
Hall Green Secondary School,
Birmingham

Mysterious Woods

It was dead of the night. The two girls were camping. Jane was putting out the campfire. Unexpectedly Lucy heard a curious noise. It was a familiar sound. Right away Lucy leapt out of the tent.

'It's Bushy!' yelled Lucy. 'He's run away into the woods!'

Jane and Lucy quickly packed up all their belongings, they switched on their torches and set off into the thick, black, dark woods.

Thump!

'Who was that?' muttered Jane.

'My torch has fallen down into the mud!' said Lucy.

'And now mine is not working!' moaned Jane.

Jane and Lucy didn't have a clue where they were going, it was as if there was nothing left in the world. Then suddenly Jane saw a hint of light glowing like a light bulb from a distance. They both started to creep towards the shiny light, which looked like a glow-worm! When they reached there they found a green, slimy, sticky trail leading deeper and deeper into the woods … they followed the slimy trail through the thick woods.

Suddenly they stopped. There seemed to be a problem, the trail split into two, one was leading to the left and the other to the right. *Oh no,* thought Lucy to herself.

After a while they decided to split up.

Lucy got really scared of the darkness surrounding her and was going to jump out of her skin, but she still carried on her journey. Jane was terrified of creepy-crawlies but she also carried on.

After all the trouble Lucy and Jane met up at the far end of the woods. They were so glad to see each other again. But there was something really strange and spooky! There was a deep, hollow hole in the ground next to Jane. Jane stepped forward and looked inside the hole. Then she screamed and yelled with horror and shock!

'What is it?' asked Lucy shivering. 'Wait, don't tell me it's our *dog*!' said Lucy in a state of alarm.

But it was worse! it was horrifying for Lucy when she heard what it was. 'Why … why? Who would do such a thing?' cried Lucy wiping her tears.

'I don't know, but we'd better get back, it's our dog's skeleton lying in there and we might also be in danger too,' answered Jane crying and sniffing.

Before they could run they saw an enormous green creature with four razor-sharp, pointed teeth and huge red eyeballs. It appeared

from behind the long, dark trees. The two girls tried to escape by taking a long step back, but when they looked down they noticed that they were stuck in the gooey slime, and were sinking down deep under the ground …

The creature came closer while the girls were speechless sinking deeper and deeper …

Sabeehah Khan (11)
Hall Green Secondary School,
Birmingham

The Grim Reaper

One dark, cold winter's night a little girl called Sophie was walking to the graveyard to put some flowers on her nan's grave. She walked over to the gravestone next to her nan and leant on it. Suddenly, the gravestone moved and it was a trapdoor! She slowly slithered down through the trapdoor to see what was lurking down there, when suddenly she saw a big red door being guarded by two Grim Reapers with their blades of steel. She was in trouble because the Grim Reapers saw her and slowly started to come at her. She slowly stepped backwards, scared stiff, but she wasn't fast enough and the Grim Reapers came forward and sliced her into two pieces. Her brother Billy, had heard her and came to look for her but little did he know that he was going to be the *next to die!*

Billy wandered around the graveyard trying to find his sister but he couldn't find her anywhere … He started to get scared when he saw his sister's dead body lying on the floor next to a grave, which had her name on it. He looked over and he saw a gravestone with his name on it too! Billy started to run when he tripped and fell down through the trapdoor. He was at the big red door and it was open, so he decided to go through it. He had done the wrong thing because he had just entered the real *Hell!*

Billy started to walk around and he tried to figure out where he was but suddenly, he knew because standing in front of him was the Devil and the two Grim Reapers that were guarding the big red door.

Billy got so scared, he tripped and hit his head on the floor. Billy opened his eyes and he thought that he was dreaming but he pinched himself and he felt it, so he knew that he wasn't dreaming. The Devil and the Grim Reapers were coming at him when he knew this was the end. However, at that moment, there was a bright flash of light and he disappeared. All he could see were bright lights and an outline of someone. It was Sophie and she was an angel but he was an angel too. This means that he was dead too and that he was in Heaven. He was so upset that he was dead but at least he was going to be with his sister for the rest of eternity and maybe for even longer …

Gareth Morris (11)
Hall Green Secondary School, Birmingham

The Possessed Boy

Darkness began to fall and the clouds drew up together squeezing out rain. Bolts of lightning shattered the rooftops. The boy was fast asleep. Suddenly his bed rapidly started to shake. The boy woke up terrified, when a white spirit hit him hard on his chest. Suddenly the boy's blue eyes turned a bloody red colour. His face went all scabby and ugly. There was a look of terror on his face that was flabbergasting. You could tell by his body language and the fire in his eyes that he was out to kill . . .

In the early hours of the next morning the boy went down to eat his breakfast. His mum noticed that he was a bit off colour. She asked him what was wrong and he answered with a fierce growl. His mum was his first victim. The boy approached, smiling, but then he grabbed her neck sharply and shoved her in the corner of the room. At that point he ripped her vital organs out and there was nothing left off her except her scream!

After he'd got into the mood of killing people, he started on his next victim. His sister. He crept into her bedroom and hid under her bed with a bread knife. His sister then felt a trickle of blood coming down by the side of her face. She looked back and saw her brother. He looked scary and fierce. She tried to run but her brother grabbed her by the neck. The girl took the nearest thing that was closest to her, an ink pen.

She grabbed it with a tight grip and squirted the pen in her brother's eyes.

She ran to the door, got out and locked it. She ran to her older brother. They both locked the doors and left the house. The boy had his mobile on him and he rang the operator for the mental asylum's number and told them to go to St Agnes Road, Hall Green, Birmingham. They arrived within five minutes with two vans and one lorry. They took the boy and put chains on his hand. At this point you could hear the ghost torturing him inside. The boy was talking as if someone was hitting him, then his older brother Sam, explained that the only way to take the ghost out of his body was to perform a ceremony, which would get the Devil out of him.

It eventually came out but it took four hours because it was at the mental asylum. You could actually see the ghost but it was in peace at last. They then moved in with their dad because their parents were divorced. They all lived happily ever after. Or did they?

Shyam Karavadra (11)
Hall Green Secondary School, Birmingham

The Mysterious Mansion

(An Extract)

Half seven it said on the flyer. That's when it all started, the day we all agreed to go. Sasha, Tina and I all got ready at Tanya's house. We were all raring to have a fun night out. Taj and the others came to pick us up, so we arrived together. It was quite weird that a party was held in the old mansion that no one ever dreamed of going to but, as nearly half of our college was attending, we thought we might as well go too.

We drove into the dark, misty pathway; the gates creaked as they opened. We parked the car near the back of the mansion so it was easier for us to exit.

We were all nervous and quiet as we walked towards the big, wooden oak door. The excited feeling faded away and soon became a sinister feeling. Taj bravely knocked on the door and took a big step back. All of us waited anxiously for someone to let us in. After what seemed five minutes, the door opened but no one was to be seen, strange? So we just went inside and *bam*! the door shut. We took our coats off and made our way into the lounge. It was beautifully decorated with banners, only a few people were there and they told us that we were early.

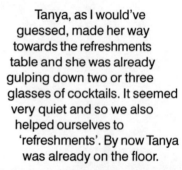

Tanya, as I would've guessed, made her way towards the refreshments table and she was already gulping down two or three glasses of cocktails. It seemed very quiet and so we also helped ourselves to 'refreshments'. By now Tanya was already on the floor.

Gradually people started coming in as we recognised some familiar faces seen in college. We did wonder who actually invited us to the party and how those posters got around the college as we didn't even know anyone who lived here or in the area.

We wanted to know, but it was very hard as no one knew. It was very strange; we didn't even know why there was a party. I suddenly felt a buzz in my back pocket and knew I had someone calling me. I went to a room where I checked who was ringing me. Surprisingly enough it was Jass!

'What you up to, Jass?' I asked.

'Yeah I'm good, how's the party going? Well, I hope all is well and you're enjoying yourself. I just wanted to tell you, have fun but take care of yourself and make sure you get home safely, okay honey?'

'Awww you're a sweetie, but I can look after myself, don't worry about me, I'm with the others. It's a shame you couldn't make it though.'

'I know but I'll see you tomorrow in college, so take care and say hi to the others.'

'You too!' I said.

I put away my phone but as I was about to leave the room I sensed someone was watching me; I turned around to check, but no one was there. Just empty, silly me, always imagining things but then the painting on the wall was as if its eyes were fixed on me. I could no longer stay in the room.

I hurried my way out except the handle wouldn't turn. I was getting very frustrated now; I tried to keep myself calm. I banged furiously on the door hoping someone would hear me …

Priya Mistry (15)
Hall Green Secondary School,
Birmingham

Horror Story

(An Extract)

The cold night froze everything in sight. I couldn't see much as the dreaded weather of November set in. I began to get worried as I was the only soul to be seen on the road. Or was I? Was there something else there?

I started to run, rapidly getting nearer and nearer to my home, I stopped at the side of the road. While I paused to take a deep breath I heard a bang. I looked all around me to see if anyone was there. When I looked around, I saw the silhouette of a man with an axe! He gradually began walking towards me. As he came towards me, I wondered who he was. What did he want?

I decided to run. I ran as fast as my legs would take me, but it was no use, he kept up with every move I took. The dead night made the road seem like it would never end. I carried on running; it felt like time was at a standstill. I began looking back to see where he was, but he had disappeared; gone as if he was never really there. Once I saw that he was gone, I took a minute to get my breath back. When I turned my head to see where I was going, he was there. A tall, dark-looking creature stood before me, I was stunned. The night was getting colder and colder. It was so quiet you could hear the daunting screams of the dead; the creature was like a man but with the head of a wolf. I was terrified. What was he going to do? I froze like a statue, not moving an inch.

I stood in front of the creature anxious and scared of what he might do, the creature appeared to be creepy and frightening. My whole body was shaking, I was so scared. I stood for a moment, until the creature moved. It came to me with a blood-filled axe in his hand; the axe already had blood on it. This made me feel concerned, I think the creature had come across someone else already; and the blood on the axe was theirs. The creature grabbed me, it didn't give me a chance to get away, it was too fast; like the speed of light. It began choking me, I could not breathe or shout for help; shouting would never help as the roads were isolated. I was all alone with this creature. Did anyone know where it was from or how it came to have the head of a wolf? I didn't know. I tried my very best to fight back, the creature was too strong, like it had the strength of ten men. This unknown creature felt unstoppable until it stopped, it no longer had me in its grasp. I was very puzzled, why did it stop? Someone else was there, watching; as if it was on TV.

The person who was there did not seem scared of the creature at all, it seemed to me, like they had met each other before. The creature and the mysterious person came up to me; the strange individual was no longer a person. It too became a beast. When the beast came into the bright, overpowering light of the moon; it transformed completely. They both took hold of me and held me in the dazzling lit moon, I felt sick; I was turning into something. My whole body felt hot, blistering; like there was a heatwave. Behind the trees there was a lake, I could see myself changing into some kind of animal …

Kulwinder Bhamber (14)
Hall Green Secondary School,
Birmingham

You Never Know Who's Out There ...

(An Extract)

'You walking the long way today?' asked Becky.

'Yeah. My mum's working late so I might meet up with my boyfriend,' replied Dimple.

'Are you sure? Look how dark it is. You never know who's out there,' Becky said, joking about. Dimple giggled as she walked to the school gates.

Walking through the foggy atmosphere, Dimple struggled to see if she was going in the right direction. She felt a breeze on her shoulder, as if someone had breathed on her. She turned around. No one was there. Laughing it off, Dimple carried on walking.

It started to get cold and dark. Dimple zipped up her coat and started to walk faster. She has this funny feeling that someone was watching her. No one, absolutely no one was there. It was not Dimple. She was the only one on the street, walking in the dark, misty night.

'You ought to get home deary. Your mother will be wondering where you are.' An old croaky voice appeared from nowhere.

Dimple jumped as an old lady came out of her house to collect her cat. 'You never know who's out there,' she continued.

Dimple smiled at the old lady and carried on walking.

The sky was getting darker. Dimple felt as if she was walking in circles. She couldn't get home. She felt lost and scared and regretted going home the long way. Water filled her eyes. Her mascara smudged as a tear rolled down her skin. She wiped it away and carried on walking …

Ring! Ring! Ring! Ring! Her phone started to ring. Dimple jumped once again. She was scared to pick up the phone. 'Hello. Oh, hey, Justin. You scared me!' With a sigh of relief, Dimple was happy to have picked up her phone to her boyfriend, just to find out that he couldn't make it.

'Get home quick babes. You never know who's out there.'

Dimple laughed and put the phone down. She started to walk faster now. She could feel the same awkward feeling that someone was watching her. To keep herself occupied, she started singing. She started to feel better.

Whilst she sang and walked, she heard the tapping of someone's shoes, as if someone was walking behind her. She stopped singing. She did not want to turn around. She could still hear the tapping of shoes behind her. They were getting louder and louder as she walked closer and closer to the never-ending journey home. Dimple turned around … no one was there.

Sonam Chauhan (14)
Hall Green Secondary School, Birmingham

Short Horror Story

(An Extract)

One frosty morning as she lay there in her bed, her sight was a cheerless, dull sky like a gloomy shadow. There was an inhuman spirit stirring in the atmosphere. It seemed to have whispered in the wind. This set her heartbeat racing. Everything in her room just reminded her of unfortunate events of her past. The red walls the colour of her sister's blood and the bars on her window of her father's prison-spent years.

She tried to shrug off all the bad feelings she was having and decided to hop into the shower. She had very distinguishing features, green eyes, a pearly white smile and often wore unusual earrings.

Just as she stepped into the shower there was a massive bang! Tara froze with fear, what was that noise? Something was not right, her stomach was filled with butterflies, she was shaking all over, full of anxiety. She quickly rushed downstairs in her towel with her bright blonde, wet hair waving all over the place. She had a massive sigh of relief, all it was, was the mail. She just searched through each letter and package and unusually there was one for her, it read 'Miss Tara Reid'. She opened it with great haste to see what the content inside revealed. Inside there was a DVD, this was very weird.

She immediately put the DVD into the player. As she nervously waited to see what the content of the DVD was, she still just sat there in her towel with her hair dripping. She was shivering but she wasn't sure if this was because of the cold weather or the fear of watching a simple disc. The disc seemed to jerk and not run smoothly - was this a sign of things to come? She was not willing to find out so she shut off the DVD player and ran straight upstairs. Just the thought of being alone scared her to death.

She rang her friend Jojo to see if they could meet up for lunch, they went to eat pizza.

'What's bothering you? You've barely touched your food,' pondered Jojo.

'It's just this weird package I got, it's a DVD but it's freaky, I don't want to watch it,' replied Tara.

'What are we waiting for; let's go watch this so called scary DVD!' As Jojo jumped out of her seat and grabbed Tara's hand as they ran back to Tara's house.

They both sat on the brown leather sofa agonisingly waiting for the DVD to start up, again it jerked. They both held each other's hand. The screen lit up with a bright white light. A creepy silhouette took shape onto the screen, they couldn't make out what it was, it appeared to be of an inhuman figure. Slowly from the feet upwards the creature was beginning to become revealed. The feet were very hairy like that of a bear, but the unusual thing was both legs were different. One was that of Godzilla's leg and the other was a peg leg with rotting wood and woodlice. As the camera moved up it had a hook arm and a human arm. The scariest feature it had was its face, it was so horrible you could not imagine. Its cheeks were brutally scarred, the forehead with some sort of skin disorder and oil burns beneath the arms. It had very sharp teeth, almost like a shark and its eyes were red. The screen began to flicker. Its last words were 'Pow!' The television suddenly switched off. The power from the whole house had gone.

Then they heard a knock at the door …

Bhavesh Tank (15)
Hall Green Secondary School,
Birmingham

The Whispers

(An Extract)

'It wasn't me!' I protested for the first few weeks. Then I stopped saying it. I wasn't to know he was a dodgy, cruel and cold-hearted person. It could've happened to anyone. At night when the lights go out, the whispers start. A very unusually spooky whisper, a bit like a scream, drifts to my small ears and makes me tingle. A scream full of pain. I can't take it anymore, I have been through too much already. Again I try to run away from these life threatening whispers, driving furiously in my small green car.

Baaannnggg! Another car accident and the same old hospital. Everyone knows my state, it's nothing new. Doctors always said I needed a break, a holiday or something. So as always me and my friends went to our farmhouse.

Deep into the darkest forest stood our old, creepy farmhouse. We drove past this deserted island. Silence, not even a bird in sight. Well anyway, on this mysterious night we set up a campfire. We needed some more wood for the fire. Becky, my best friend, went rushing into the mysterious, dark forest. She'd always loved campfires. Time flew by very quickly and there was no sign of Becky. She couldn't be seen in this horrible, dark forest. Curious to find Becky, Jon and Ben went into the forest to look for her.

As they put their feet onto the forest soil they felt a sharp coldness rise into their bodies. They felt as it someone was following them. It was just their conscience. The wind started to blow faster and furiously. They both looked for Becky but couldn't find her anywhere. Suddenly Becky appeared out of nowhere in a very unusual way. Ben and Jon looked at her: they didn't know what had happened to her. They were extremely confused. A split second later Becky started screaming but mysteriously it wasn't her voice and she looked furious. Panicking, Ben and Jon got her out of there. Without telling anyone they took her away from the forest.

Doctors couldn't work out what was wrong with her. Whenever they did an X-ray of Becky nothing showed up. There was another problem, she didn't react to anything. She became very dangerous and hard to handle. They could see another soul inside her, screaming in pain. Eventually she died.

Marya Hussain (15)
Hall Green Secondary School, Birmingham

The Woman In The Mirror

Lucy and her family went to an antique shop and each of them bought something, Lucy choosing a big old mirror. So they went home and took the mirror with them. Lucy put the mirror up in the attic where her bedroom was.

A couple of days later she invited her friend Beth over to sleep. Lucy and Beth were downstairs sleeping when Beth got up to go and get her blanket. She reached the attic and had a look in Lucy's new mirror but she didn't see her face …

There was a pale face with long, black, loose hair.

'Lucy, Lucy look there's someone in the mirror!'

'Don't be silly, there's nothing,' Lucy replied.

Lucy couldn't see the figure but Beth knew what she'd seen.

Later on Beth heard screams from upstairs in the attic so she ran to see what it was.

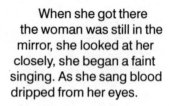

When she got there the woman was still in the mirror, she looked at her closely, she began a faint singing. As she sang blood dripped from her eyes.

'Arrggh!' Beth screamed and ran downstairs, she knew there was no point telling Lucy, she didn't believe her.

Beth couldn't get to sleep she could still hear the pale woman singing.

She crept slowly upstairs and stepped into the attic.

'What do you want with me? Leave me alone, stop haunting me,' said Lucy.

'Well you won't have to worry about that anymore,' she whispered.

'Why?' Beth looked puzzled.

She was never seen again!

Suzanne Elsdon (10)
Healey Primary School, Rochdale

The Chained Ghost

He slammed the door behind him, ran across the wooden floor and hid behind an old, stained rocking chair. A loud clunking noise came up the stairs, it sounded like chains rattling. There was a loud groaning noise coming from behind the door. A ghostly white hand appeared through the door, then the rest of the body appeared. The boy screamed. The figure approached him, but as soon as he got to him the figure disappeared.

The boy was traumatised. He told his parents, but they ignored him, when he returned to his room there were ghostly footprints where the ghost had been. But when he took another glance, the footprints led to his wardrobe. The boy paced the room slowly, and the floorboards began to creak again. He reached out his shaking hand and grasped the doorknob and slowly began to turn it, he tugged on the stiff door, it creaked open. There in front of him was a sight he never wanted to see again.

A body that had a slit on its neck, it was the ghostly figure he had seen, only this time he was a real person! The boy went as white as the ghost he had just seen. The body stepped out of the wardrobe and he pulled out of his pocket a short, rusty dagger. He pierced the boy's flesh with the dagger.

Now from this day on if you hear a heartless groaning coming from the house on the hill, it's the boy.

Rachel Harrop (11)
Healey Primary School,
Rochdale

Spooks In The House

In the middle of Stropford, there was a large house that no one lived in. It had cobwebs on the windows and spiders lived in the door frames where it had cracked a lot.

One night, a few girls were having a sleepover and one of the girls, named Suzy, peered out of the window and caught a glimpse of the house and suddenly couldn't take her eyes off the house.

Early next morning, Suzy got up before all of her friends and went looking for the house.

When she found the house she knocked on the door. She felt as if no one could hurt her. When no one answered the door, she took a breath and opened the door and stepped inside.

She found her way up some really creaky stairs and into a bedroom. It was very preserved and there was a bell on the bed.

Suzy moved into the next room and saw something blurred and then heard a laugh. In this room there was a fireplace and the fire was blazing to light the room. Then suddenly from the next room, she heard a bell ring. On the third ring, the fire went out and the door shut.

At this time, her friends awoke and ran to tell Suzy's parents that she'd gone.

Well Suzy was getting frightened by now, so she ran for the door. When she reached out for the door, something pulled her back and she was never seen again, neither was the house, and with that my story ends.

Sophie Young (10)
Healey Primary School, Rochdale

The Deadly Easter Bunny

Easter was approaching and everyone was happy except for the Easter bunny! He was a murderer and he wanted to carry on his work this Easter.

Last Easter he had killed 12 people and his sidekick, the Easter elf, had killed 2 people and seriously injured someone.

An egg hunt was going to happen so the Easter bunny went.

A child was coming towards him shouting, 'I've found one, I've found one.'

As soon as he was near the bush the Easter bunny got a knife out and that was the end of the little child.

There was a shriek. People ran as fast as they could and found the dead child. What they didn't know was when they were looking at the child, the Easter elf had got into a car and was coming straight at them.

The car was a Ferrari Enzo and it was going at top speed. It hit the people and when the window wipers had wiped off the blood he saw how many people were dead.

They carried on but the police saw them and chased them. They got caught and locked up.

That was the end of the Easter bunny and the Easter elf and the boy they killed haunted them for the rest of their short lives.

Two years later when they died they had babies called Mini Easter bunny and Easter Elf Jnr.

They carried on their dads' work and killed more people but that's a different story altogether.

Matthew Sexton (10)
Healey Primary School, Rochdale

Christmas Eve

It was Christmas Eve, snow was falling and children were building snowmen. Ryan Collier was the name of a snowman. The children lived in the town of Choovill. Ryan Collier lived next to a graveyard.

The Wood family had spent ages building Ryan. Ryan had a carrot for his nose and two stones for his eyes and buttons for his mouth.

Michael told his children it was time to go to bed so Patrick and Gary went to bed but Ryan was really a ghost who scared all the children and when Michael walked out of the children's room he heard a scream. He ran back in and he saw Ryan floating around the room going, 'Whoooo!'

The children were screaming their heads off so Michael picked up a baseball bat and tried to hit Ryan over the head and said, 'Bye-bye Ryan the snowman, I have wanted to do this for ages and now I can!' He swung and swung but Ryan was too fast, the children were hiding under their duvet covers.

Then Michael's wife came stomping upstairs and saw him hitting thin air with a baseball bat. 'What are you doing?' she said sharply.

'Can't you see the ghost?' he explained.

'Ghost!' she said and started to laugh.

'Oh well!' He stopped and went to bed.

Next morning the kids woke up and Ryan Collier was nowhere to be seen at all.

Michael Wood (10)
Healey Primary School, Rochdale

I Have To Escape

I used to be a news reporter, finding every decent story I could get. Then I did find a story, one that could have elevated my career.

Standing on a box at the seaman's mission peering through a small window, I was staring in wonder at three women chanting round a book. It was open with a small gold bowl next to it, this was bubbling. They chucked in a little bottle full of liquid that was unrecognisable from my distance, into the bowl. Then something ran across my foot, I shuffled my feet quickly while cursing and fell through the box. The women looked up when I just managed to scramble to my feet.

'Vangour del les shouque toci,' I heard. A green transparent creature appeared in front of me and I ran through it. The women looked up again and came out of the shelter, one of them raised a hand and a blue ball erupted from her hand and she fired it at me, but missed.

I came here to Chicago, with a curse because I ran through the creature. The curse will hang over me forever.

Joseph Bootham (11)
Healey Primary School, Rochdale

Trapped!

Jessica knew that as soon as she reached up to knock on Chloe's new house's front door, she was in deep trouble. Like as soon as you let Dracula into your house. Except that she wasn't the Dracula …

Chloe rushed to the door as soon as Jessica's hand reached the knocker. *There's something different about her*, Jess thought. *Her eyes are like shining steel and they follow you wherever you tread.*

Jess couldn't seem to concentrate on whatever Chloe did with her. She was thinking about Chloe. Chloe never used to be like that. Jess was drawn to her eyes and couldn't look away. Then Chloe's eyes changed. They went red and colours like fireworks sparkled across them. They went into all shades of any colour and Jess was entranced.

Hypnotised is another word but plainly, her mind went blank and no thoughts could creep in whatsoever. She fell into a deep, deep sleep and would not wake up for anything.

Her dream was of a horrible kind. She was in a dark, damp maze. She thought she could see a light in front of her but never reached it. After lots of twisting and turning in the maze, she heard a scream. Now she was really scared. She rushed about in the maze and she prayed to God for her to wake up.

God must have listened because she woke up.

But this was scarier now. A pale-faced man with an upturned collar was slowly walking towards her …

Lydia Bruton-Jones (10)
Healey Primary School,
Rochdale

The Crying From The Room

It was Lucy's first night in the new house and she just couldn't sleep. At about 3am she went to get a drink. But as she crossed the landing, she heard a sort of crying noise from the strange little room at the end of the landing.

Nobody should be there? She was quite scared so she went back to bed.

When she went downstairs the next day, she only saw Dad.

'So you're finally up then.'

'Yes, but where's Mum?'

'What do you mean? It's always been just you and me.'

She was quite confused and when she looked at the family photo in the hall, she was horrified to see that her mum's picture had disappeared.

The next day seemed to last a lifetime. Lucy was alone with nobody to tell her what was happening.

In the afternoon, she was standing at the window of the strange, little room. She looked outside and heard some builders talking.

'It's a shame that old house burnt down. A new family had just moved in when it happened,' said one of the builders to the other.

'They say they were asleep. They say they died in their beds. Some people say they have heard crying from the house.'

And with these words, Lucy had finally found out what happened. She was a ghost. As a tear trickled down her cheek, she saw her flesh disappear.

'Did you hear that? It sounded like someone was crying. It came from the house!'

Nicholas Watkins (14)
Lakelands School & Sports College,
Ellesmere

The House Of Death

I was living in my new house. It was lovely but I thought it looked very dull on the outside. Nobody really talked to us or went out in the sun.

On my third week I went to Bay Cliff School. I imagined it would be beautiful but it was dark, gloomy, icy and cobwebs hung from the ceilings.

As soon as I arrived everyone stared at me. I stood in shock after about ten minutes I woke up out of the daze and walked towards the headmaster's office. It was the same as every other room but with lots of books and papers.

The headmaster stared at me and said, 'Who are you?'

'Tanya,' I said.

'The new girl, you're in Class 6,' he said. 'Hurry up or you'll miss registration.'

When I got to class, everyone stared at me again. I just ignored them and sat down and did my work.

At break time we had to stay in the dark and gloomy classroom because we weren't allowed out to play. Besides nobody wanted to go out except me, of course.

At four o'clock, I arrived home. 'School was weird,' I said to Mum.

'What?' she said.

Saturday I invited my cousins over. We were talking, I heard a knock on the door, answered it and saw lots of people.

'What do you want?' I said.

'You and your cousins,' they replied.

I ran into Sarah and Louise and said, 'We've got to go.'

'Why?' they asked.

'See for yourselves.'

They did.

I followed and saw Sarah on the ground with a bite mark on her neck, then a trail of blood caught my eye, it led to a nearby house.

On the door it said *Beware Of The Blood-Sucking Vampires* written in the blood I had seen. The door opened, I went in and saw Louise change into a skeleton . . .

Tanya McCullagh (11)
St Columban's Primary School, Belcoo

Ghost Story

My brother Jamie and I were going for a stroll down the road. We saw a mysterious house. We thought it was haunted so we went in. I told my brother to stay at the gate.

In the house there was a stove on, I thought that was very unusual. I went upstairs. The sweat was running off me. I managed to get out of the hole in the staircase.

I continued upstairs, there were clean sheets on the beds.

I went over to the other bedrooms and there were clean sheets on those beds too.

I turned around and the door shut and there were no windows open when I first went in there.

I went over and I could hear the other doors creaking but I never heeded.

I saw a shadow, I turned round, the shadow was gone! My heart was pumping like mad, it was like I was going to have a heart attack.

I opened the door and there was an old lady. I asked, 'What is your name?'

She replied, 'My name is Miriam.'

I said, 'My name is Linda and my brother outside is called Jamie. I have to go now, it's getting late.'

She said, 'Bye.'

I walked outside and went home with my brother Jamie.

I never saw her again. She must have been a ghost!

Linda McGovern (10)
St Columban's Primary School, Belcoo

Horror

Three children in a park appears a happy situation, but this was not. The Smiths were being told that their parents were consumed in the flames of the 'Happy-Go Lucky' restaurant; they felt like 'experiment-gone-wrong children'.

Sarah, Harry and Colleen Smith had been running cheerfully in Oak Park when Mr Damen, their babysitter, told them a man ran in and set the restaurant on fire.

The children blamed themselves as they encouraged their parents to celebrate their anniversary.

Colleen broke the silence, saying, 'Who takes custody of us now?'

'Your cousin from Oklahoma.'

'We don't have a cousin in Oklahoma!'

The conversation continued like this before they went home.

When the children woke up their cheeks were stiff, their pillows wet; they had been grieving all night long. Now they had to leave.

Arriving in Oklahoma Damie gave them Snickers; being allergic to nuts they threw them away.

Their cousin arrived half an hour late, wearing the most ridiculous outfit ever. His car was a catastrophe.

'Hello mates!' he said.

'Hi,' they replied.

Next morning they asked Ollie where Damie was.

'Gone,' he replied.

But his car was still outside. There was something fishy about Ollie.

That evening they were going to a restaurant in the car when they noticed Colleen bouncing on a bulge.

In the restaurant their minds were working overtime; when Harry saw a girl throw something, he remembered the Snickers.

He whispered to Sarah and they ordered peanuts and got horrible rashes. They ran to the car, found Damie's body, phoned the police and Ollie was arrested.

Sinéad O'Donovan (10)
St Columban's Primary School, Belcoo

A Ghost Story

One dark evening, a boy went for a walk. He heard a terrifying whisper behind him. He looked behind and started to walk again, but a man stood in front of him. The man chased him and his face started melting. He grew a long cloak then had a skeleton face and was holding a bloody axe. It was the Grim Reaper.

He ran to hide in a nearby shed, but skeletons rose up out of the floor. The Grim Reaper came through the wall. The boy screamed and ran out of the door, but the skeletons were quicker. Then the Grim Reaper came and threw him a note. It fell on the ground. The skeletons melted into the ground. The Grim Reaper vanished in a cloud of dark smoke.

The boy picked up the note. It said, 'Come to the haunted house at the end of your road at 12 tonight, or your friend gets it!' The note was written in blood.

At twelve he went to the house and through the creaking front door. He went into a room and saw his friend. He gave a loud shriek because his friend was holding his head in front of him. The mouth opened and said, 'Come, join us!' and out of the wall came lots of headless bodies, holding their heads. Before the boy knew it, the Grim Reaper had used his bloody axe to cut off the boy's head. He was now one of them.

Clodagh McMorrow (10)
St Columban's Primary
School, Belcoo

Tu-whit Tu-whoo, Bang!

It was a dark, spooky, stormy night, I was in my granny's house. I went up to bed. I could see the shadows of branches blowing about, hitting the windows through the blinds. They were like sharp, spread out claws of demons looking through the window.

I was walking over to the bed and I heard a noise! I stood still. The noise was like a ghost breathing heavily. Was it a ghost? I didn't really believe in ghosts. Suddenly I heard the tu-whit tu-whoo of an owl and the flapping of wings, almost like the sound of a machine gun. Then I heard a thump, followed by a loud scream. I jumped up and ran downstairs to my granny.

There she was, standing still and breathing heavily. She was staring out of the window. We went outside to check what had happened. A huge owl was lying there.

So that's what had happened! An owl had flown into the window and my granny screamed because she had seen it falling down.

Paul McNulty (10)
St Columban's Primary School, Belcoo

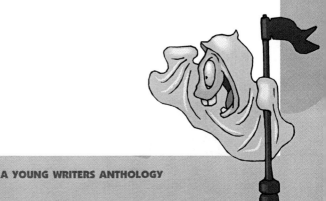

Strange Happenings

Bang! The front of the car was rendered useless. Another gunshot rang out, taking out the right rear wheel. They were heading for the oil rigs!

Chris shouted, 'Bail out!' and everyone jumped fearlessly, landing on a soft patch of grass. The sniper ran down the hill and just vanished into thin air.

Chris, John, Paul, Aaron and Ian were shocked that someone could disappear like that. They had stopped at an abandoned house near the small village of Crickhollow, 30 miles away.

Eventually Ian said, 'Where's Ciaran?' They heard a faint grunt. Then they saw the injured body of Ciaran, scalded by the fire as he jumped out last and landed on the concrete. Ian volunteered to stay with him and call the ambulance.

Chris, John, Paul and Aaron came back with some wild fruits. They noticed that Ciaran and Ian were missing. They were scared as they explored the abandoned house. They split up.

Chris heard a mighty crack. He ran out to the hallway and found out what had happened.

When the police arrived they kicked the door in. Aaron had tripped over and got caught in a creeper. Ciaran and Ian went to the hospital. The sniper slipped and whacked his head on a stone and was unconscious. John Paul had fallen through a floorboard.

Suddenly furniture of all manner came flying towards them. Only three were injured and when everything was wrapped up, Chris asked the police what was in the house. They said that the owner had died years ago, he liked being noisy and hurtful as he was a poltergeist. From then on they watched where they set foot.

Patrick Sweeney (10)
St Columban's Primary School, Belcoo

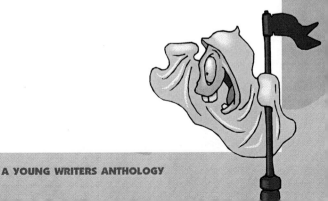

The Dark Shadow

I cycled to my friend's house for a sleepover. We were playing in her room when I left to go to the toilet. I was washing my hands when the water went off and the light started flashing. The toilet began flushing by itself and then a shadow formed on the wall. It seemed to look like the *Devil!*

I ran out to my friend's room. She was gone! Then I ran to her mother, father and brother's rooms but they were gone too! I saw the Shadow again. I went into the hall and tried to phone for help but the phone line was down. The electric was out. I tried my mobile to call for help but it fell into the sink which still had water in it. I then tried to use my friend's mobile. It was in the kitchen, but the battery was dead so I ran into a cupboard to hide.

I was there for two hours with no sign of the 'shadow'.

I thought it was safe, so I crept out of the cupboard into the hall to see if there was any sign of the 'shadow'. I walked slowly all around the house but there was no sign of it.

When I got back to the hall, I ran out of the front door to my bike and I cycled in the dark, through the spooky field but suddenly the shadow reappeared . . .

Tamara McGourty (10)
St Columban's Primary
School, Belcoo

The 31st

It was 10.15am on a gloomy hill in the middle of the United States of America.

In the pure black sky of darkness shone hundreds and hundreds of night-time stars, on Friday the 31st of October. John and his neighbour Michael were down in the barn making sure that the cows were alright, when suddenly the bar door smashed shut behind them. They thought that it was the wind, but was it … ? A headless man who was supposed to have been terrorising the village for weeks was hidden in the barn.

He stalked John as he walked towards the cows and as John turned round, he was stabbed. He screamed in distress as the headless man pulled the knife out. Michael tried to escape but the door was jammed. He was forced into a corner but just when the headless man was about to stab Michael, John's dad heard their screams and ran up to the barn with his shotgun. He came through a hole in the old barn's wall. He aimed his gun and shot at the wall behind the headless man, leaving a big hole for the headless man to escape through.

He had already killed John which left the whole village melancholy. There was no way that the town was going to get over this sad and horrifying event. No one knew when the mysterious murderer would pick out his next poor victim or on which night and at what time would the headless man strike again?

Victims, rest in peace.

Séimí Rafferty (10)
St Columban's Primary School,
Belcoo

The Spooky Manor

I live in a house and just across the hill there is a two-storey manor. It's very spooky. At midnight every night, there's a horse-drawn carriage with what looks like a man with no head, driving it. It goes up the stony lane and as soon as it stops, the driver's gone in a cloud of black smoke fumes.

One day I was out playing football when I kicked the ball over the fence and onto the street of the manor. When I went to get it, I just ran and picked it up and then ran home. When I got home, I told my mom where I'd been and she said, 'If that ever happens again, you'll be grounded!'

Unfortunately, we found out, since we had only just come to live here, the owner of the manor across the hill, was our landlord. When we went to pay, my mother was so scared. A man with no head came, and my mom said, 'Where's the closest beach?' He pointed to the left and mom ran into the car and drove away very quickly.

The next day we went back to pay the rent and the man with no head came to the door again and Mom said, 'I'm here to pay the rent.'

'Will you be paying cash or cheque for the rent?' he said. My mom dropped the money and ran - because the man had no head.

Anthony Mulvey (10)
St Columban's Primary
School, Belcoo

The Dreadful Chase

'What are we going to do? We're trapped!' Tom snapped as he ran. He was running like the fastest thing on Earth.

'If we don't move faster, we'll be salami kalami! Oooppss! The ground is shaking!'

By now they were running five kilometres an hour. The ground had already started shaking rapidly. It was like being in an earthquake! Gradually, the footsteps were to be heard, louder and louder. Shaggy started struggling, he couldn't keep running!

'Quick, find a solution!' whispered Tom.

Zzzzooinkks! I think I'm a banana! thought Shaggy. They both struggled to keep up the speed. Suddenly Shaggy had an idea to hide in the corner of the tunnel, but Tom doubted him. Luckily they saw the end of the tunnel.

By now they were on land and finally the dinosaur started slowing down.

'Hey, what's this? A map! Okay, let's follow it and then we can find our way out.'

They followed the instructions and the title was 'How To Control Dinosaurs'. It said if you show a torch to the magnifying glass and show it in the dinosaur's eyes, you could control it. Then Tom saw the materials needed and they had everything. So he showed the torch in the dinosaur's eyes and Shaggy held the magnifying glass up to Tom and it worked. The dinosaur was blinded and finally lost its way.

'Nice work!' And they celebrated.

Akbar-Ali Bhimani (12)
St Constantine's International
School, Tanzania

The Ghost In The Haunted House

Oh my dad's got a promotion and we're going to Gingerville!

'Mum, is that the place where Emma moved to?' said Darla over the kitchen counter.

After nearly an hour, we were on the way to Gingerville. I was so excited. I was so happy that I would be in the same school as Emma! Guess what? I was going to have my own room. Wow!

That night when I went to brush my teeth I heard a baby's cry. I was surprised because we had no neighbours! I just ignored it. Then my mum called me for dinner. It was very delicious.

My mum tucked me into bed and I was soon fast asleep. Suddenly in the middle of the night, I was wide awake. I could hear footsteps, I was scared, but I just switched on the lamp and started reading my diary. After some time, the lamp started flicking on and off. I thought I was too excited with moving and meeting Emma, but I was so scared.

I went to wake my mum up and when I told her what had happened, she said I was thinking too much. Then she heard the footsteps herself!

It was dark so we tried to switch on the lights but the switches were stuck. Then we heard the car moving out of the garage. My dad went out with his gun.

When he returned from the garage, we saw a girl dressed in a white gown she had black hair and her clothes were drenched in blood.

I told my father that we should leave that house immediately, so we went to a hotel. I was fast asleep until ten in the morning, then we moved into an apartment. Though it was small I didn't mind it after that horrible experience!

Kulsoom M Sajan (11)
St Constantine's International School, Tanzania

The Key

It was eerily quiet in the tent outside Beckie's house. Suddenly she saw her friend Jenny climbing into the tent with drinks, saying, 'Your mum said we've to get into our sleeping bags, but we can talk.'

'Good, we can tell ghost stories,' Beckie said.

'G-g-g-g-ghost stories!' Jenny squeaked. 'Er … okay!'

The girls told tales about werewolves and vampires, but Jenny was scared of the story called 'The Key'. Beckie told it to Jenny.

'Thirteen years ago a vicar was attacked and killed whilst locking up his church one evening. The key to the church door was never found. It is said that the spirit of the vicar still searches the woods to this day for the key.'

'I'm tired, let's go to bed,' said Jenny.

'Okay,' said Beckie.

Beckie and Jenny got into their sleeping bags. After a while Jenny woke up because of some loud whispering outside. She got up to investigate. She opened the tent zip and saw a faint body in the distance beside a tree, whispering, 'Where's the key?'

As soon as she saw the figure coming towards her, she zipped up the tent and got back into bed as fast as she could.

In the morning, Jenny didn't mention what had happened the night before to Beckie. When Jenny got home, she ran in, saying, 'Dad, where's the key you found in the woods a fortnight ago?'

Her dad got out an old shoe box and inside it there was an old rusty key, just like in Beckie's story …

Beckie Morris (9)
St Michael's East Wickham CE (VA) Primary School,
Welling

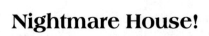

Nightmare House!

Finally, it was the day; the Jones' were moving into their new home. They had been searching for an old house for many years and found this one by chance. One day Dad took a wrong turning on the way to work and ended up driving down a very long country lane. The house was at the end of the lane. When he saw the house he fell in love with it and bought it that day.

The family pulled up into the driveway and got out of the car. He was so please that they were moving into the new house.

The removal company had already dropped off their belongings. When they got through the front door there were boxes and boxes. They had no oven so he went to the market to get food. He took a walk down to the market with his dog and his son went with him as well.

Mrs Jones was in the house by herself. She started to unpack. She was afraid in this large house, alone by herself.

The house was eerily quiet, she started shaking, she froze - it was creepy and she was scared. All of a sudden the lights went off and a tapping noise started. She turned stark white. Mrs Jones saw something out of the corner of her eye. She had her mobile phone in her pocket, so Mrs Jones dialled Mr Jones' number, but there was no signal! 'Help me please!' she said, giving a blood-curdling scream. The place was gloomy and foggy.

Mrs Jones looked for the light switch, she felt a cold hand on her back. She turned, nothing was there. She thought it was a dream. She went into the living room and as she was sitting down on one of the boxes, the box moved backwards. Mrs Jones heard a laugh.

As the door opened the lights suddenly came on. When the rest of the family came in, the lights switched off and all that was heard was a scream by the whole family.

A ghost appeared from one of the boxes. It was an old man dressed in Victorian clothes. The house was haunted! That was the reason no one had lived there for many years. The Jones family ran out of the house and never returned.

It was five years later when a new family moved in. Was the same thing going to happen to the new family?

Shannon Staines (10)
St Michael's East Wickham CE (VA) Primary School, Welling

The Choking Ghost

It was a very dark night. The rain was lashing down onto and through the broken roof tiles. Inside the attic of the old manor house lived a ghost called Joe. He was a very funny ghost and he had a friend called Mary. Mary goes to school with her best friend Elle.

The headmaster, Mr Varney, takes the assembly every day and Edward talked through it all.

After school, when Joe got home, he decided to have a biscuit that Mary and Mr Varney had made for him, but it had been in the biscuit tin a very long time. It was so hard that when he bit into it and tried to swallow, it just stuck in his throat. (Yes, he's a ghost but he does have teeth and a throat!)

He stretched his neck but it still stayed stuck in his throat. He flew into the wall and kept on doing this to try to make it go down, but it was no good as it was lodged in his throat.

Mary walked into the room and saw him, 'What are you doing?' she said to Joe.

'I'm trying to get your biscuit out of my throat!' he said.

'Here, let me help you,' she said and she put her hand through him and pulled the biscuit out!

Emma Castle (9)
St Michael's East Wickham
CE (VA) Primary School, Welling

Friday The 13th

Once a girl called Rebecca went to bed thinking about the next day which was Friday the 13th. She always hated that day because something always went wrong! She fell asleep thinking about it.

As she slept she had a dream that she was in the woods and she tripped up on a stone. She had a big cut on her face. Rebecca could see lots of shadows but couldn't see anyone. She could hear the wind whistling. Then she felt lots of cold drips, it had started to rain. It poured down. Rebecca couldn't turn back now because there was a wall in a square and Rebecca was in the middle of it.

She tried to climb up the walls but she couldn't grip on to anything.

Suddenly she felt a chill on her shoulder and she heard a blood-curdling scream and the tips of her hair stood on end, like a prickly hedgehog. She heard a voice like no other, saying, 'What are you doing here? There's no use in trying to get out, we've got you now!' She turned round and saw a white outline with a face on it. Fourteen more of them appeared. They were *ghosts!*

Then she heard another voice saying, 'Come on, quickly! Why have you slept through your alarm? You've got a school trip today.' It was only Mum.

'I kept seeing ghosts - about fifteen of them, it was like a horror film!'

Luckily it was only a dream!

Katie Crowe (9)
St Michael's East Wickham CE (VA)
Primary School, Welling

The House Nobody Wants To Live In

One day the Freeman family, their handsome dad Kevin, his beautiful wife Rebecca and their lovely daughter Katie, decided that they wanted to move house.

The next day they went to the estate agents to find a new house.

'We've got just the house for you,' said Franky Stein, the estate agent.

The house that Franky thought would be good for them, was a haunted house. Nobody had lived there for over ten years. The last person had lived there for about a week and then was never seen again!

The following day, Franky took the Freeman family to the house. When they started driving, it was sunny and warm but as they were getting closer to the mansion, the conditions were changing. There were dark clouds, they could hear thunder in the distance and they were getting chilly. 'This looks scary,' whispered Katie to her mum.

When Franky opened the door it made a terrifying, creaking sound. The house was eerily quiet.

They looked around the living room first. Kevin felt a cold breeze. 'Is it me or is it cold in here?' he asked.

'It's you!' said Katie.

Then suddenly the door slammed shut.

'What was that?' Mum yelled.

As they went up the stairs, they heard thumping footsteps and they were not even walking! They looked at each other in horror. 'Can we go home?' asked Katie.

They suddenly heard a blood-curdling scream.

'What was that?' shrieked Mum, as she started to panic.

'I want to go home,' yelled Katie.

'I think we'd better!' exclaimed Dad.

Lauren Kelly (10)
St Michael's East Wickham CE (VA) Primary School,
Welling

Dennis, Billy And The Hunchback

One night, two boys called Dennis and Billy went to the graveyard. It was pitch-black in the graveyard and they couldn't see a thing. Billy began to tease Dennis and he told Dennis that shadows were moving around the graveyard. They both had a torch but Billy's torch kept flickering off.

Dennis said, 'Billy, stop mucking about, I'm getting scared.'

Billy went missing in the graveyard. A hunchbacked man grabbed Billy.

Dennis heard noises and could see things moving, he thought, *it's still Billy mucking about trying to scare me.*

The hunchbacked man asked Billy, 'Why are you here?'

Billy ran away but he had dropped his torch and couldn't see where he was going.

Dennis kept searching for his friend. He heard a noise behind him. When he flashed his torch, he only saw shadows. He called Billy's name but Billy was too terrified to answer in case the hunchbacked man tried to catch him. Dennis then saw the hunchbacked man and realised it wasn't Billy playing games. Dennis began to worry about his friend and wondered where he was.

He found Billy's torch and wondered if Billy was still in the graveyard or had he gone home? Dennis found a tree at the back of the graveyard and climbed it so that he could decide what to do. He saw Billy creeping about and he flashed his torch at him; Billy saw the flash and went to meet Dennis, then the two friends ran home, scared!

Alex James Cormack (10)
St Michael's East Wickham CE (VA) Primary School, Welling

The Demon Who Became A Vicar

One misty night a demon called Willbert awoke and walked out of his graveyard.

'Demon!' a horrified voice shouted. Everyone ran inside, they were scared.

Willbert heard a dinging sound coming from the church. Suddenly people started coming out of the church. Willbert hid behind a tree, its branches whispered in the breeze. He saw someone wearing a long scarf. He thought, *I like his clothes, I want to be what he is* - So he went to him.

'Hello,' Willbert said.

'Oh hello!' the vicar replied. He was petrified.

Willbert had horns and black hair, his fingers were long and bony. 'I want to be like you,' said Willbert nicely.

The vicar let out a blood-curdling scream.

'Calm down, I'm a nice demon,' said Willbert.

'Come with me,' the vicar said nervously. He took him to a room to practise his Sermon.

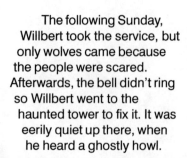

The following Sunday, Willbert took the service, but only wolves came because the people were scared. Afterwards, the bell didn't ring so Willbert went to the haunted tower to fix it. It was eerily quiet up there, when he heard a ghostly howl.

Willbert was scared, terror etched on his face. He looked at the clock and saw that there was no bell. He heard footsteps, then the creaking door slammed shut! He tried to open it. He kicked it so hard that when it opened he fell down the gloomy staircase. No one else had heard the footsteps and the bell was ringing again.

The villagers were no longer afraid of Willbert because he had scared the tower's ghost away.

Matthew Snow (10)
St Michael's East Wickham CE (VA) Primary School, Welling

The Haunted House

There was a family who had moved into the village and they knew nothing about the village.

As soon as they got there, they went looking for a house. They went to the estate agent to pick their house. They chose a house, and the good thing was that they could check out the new house straight away.

When they arrived, they were so excited. Jenny said to John, 'Why don't you go and get some food while I check the house?'

'Okay!' said John.

When Jenny walked into the house she could hear thumping upstairs so she went to investigate. When she got to the attic she couldn't see a thing because the lights were turned off. She started feeling the walls, looking for the light switch. She went to touch the light switch, but there was blood on it and she screamed. She ran over to the door and John was there. They both decided to have dinner before going back into the attic.

Jenny and John were eating and they both heard something in the attic. *Crash! Bang!* They went to the ladder which led to the attic.

Jenny and John got to the attic and the noise they'd heard was the boxes falling down. Then they both turned round and thought they saw a ghost. John said to Jenny, 'Don't worry, it's only our reflection in the mirror!'

Stephen Wickes (9)
St Michael's East Wickham
CE (VA) Primary School,
Welling

She Walks At Night

One day a new family, the Adams, moved into town. Their names were Angela and Steve and they desperately needed a house.

They found one they liked. The estate agent said, 'No one has lived in this house for more than ten years.'

They got used to the house but they kept on hearing footsteps and tapping and they also heard whispering noises, which made them worried.

It was a dark and gloomy evening and Angela said to Steve, 'I'm going to stay up for a bit and then I'll go to bed.'

'Okay love, I'm going to bed now,' replied Steve.

It got later and colder into the night. Suddenly Angela heard a faint whisper.

'Leave! Beware!' All of a sudden the door flew open and a bright light shone through. Angela looked round, terror etched on her face and at the same time she let out a blood-curdling scream.

Steve came running down the stairs wondering what all the racket was. He went into the living room and Angela was lying on the floor surrounded by a pool of blood. Steve called out, 'Angela! Angela!' but she didn't answer, she had fainted. There was a message in the blood, it said, *Leave, or else* - Steve was petrified.

When Angela came round Steve said, 'That's it, we're leaving!'

They left that night and never came back.

Shannon Summerskill (10)
St Michael's East Wickham CE (VA)
Primary School, Welling

The Haunted Castle

In the valley stood a scary-looking castle. It was the only shelter for miles so we could get out of the rain.

'Come on Charlie,' whispered Danielle.

'Not me!' said Pete.

As I opened the big wooden door it gave out a loud creak and a thunderbolt went across the sky. 'This is creepy,' said Charlie, and all our teeth started to chatter together. All we could see was darkness. Danielle found a lantern nearby.

'What are you doing?' said Pete.

'I'm trying to get this to work,' said Danielle.

The door slammed behind us and we all yelled, 'Who was that?' As the lantern began to light up, our imaginations began to run wild, thinking all sorts. We just stood there and froze.

Right ahead of us was this big, huge staircase with cobwebs as big as a house.

'I'm scared,' said Charlie.

'Ssshhh, did you hear that?' said Pete.

'Don't be silly,' said Danielle. 'Come on you chickens!'

As they began to climb the stars, the hairs on the backs of their necks began to stand on end. As they took step by step, their legs were shaking.

'Did you see that?' said Danielle.

'What? Tell us!' both Charlie and Pete said, in whispered voices. 'There it is again. Ssshhh!'

Across the landing at the top of the stairs, stood a shadow.

'Is someone there?' shouted Charlie, Pete and Danielle.

They were all shaking in terror …

Danielle Hickey (10)
St Michael's East Wickham CE (VA) Primary School,
Welling

Welcome To The Dead House

There once was a family who lived in a house. One day they decided to move, but Mrs Shuttle's children, Josh and Daniel, weren't comfortable about moving and their dog, Lucky, wasn't either. But they moved to a big house with a school just up the road.

Their estate agent, Mr Dawes, was a spirit but the Shuttle family didn't know that.

One night, Josh and Daniel's parents went to a party. Josh was in bed.

'Daniel, I'm going out to get some fresh air,' said Josh. So he went out with Daniel. Somebody grabbed them. It was Mr Dawes.

'Let me show you something,' said Mr Dawes. He took them to the cemetery.

At the cemetery there were three graves, it was their old friends, Tony, Ryan and Joe.

'But it can't be!' gasped Daniel.

Mr Dawes said, 'They're spirits like me now! I'm going to kill you!' screamed Mr Dawes.

'Get back! No!' said Daniel.

Mr Dawes was getting hurt and scratched by zombies, bats and vampires who had risen from the dead.

Josh and Daniel's parents were getting beaten up also by mysterious skeleton heads.

Josh and Daniel were out of breath. Josh was petrified looking at a skeleton head stuck on a bat's body.

'Josh are you alright now?'

So Josh said, 'Daniel!' but Daniel's words unfroze them and they both scarpered back to their house. There wasn't any more *scary stuff* for them and they were not scared of anything, anymore.

Joshua Cook (9)
St Michael's East Wickham CE (VA) Primary School, Welling

The Gruesome Graveyard

It was a dark and gloomy night and the graveyard was crawling with spirits and ghosts, as Charlie, Josh, Stephen and George opened the gate.

Charlie said, 'I don't like the look of this place.'

'Did you hear that? I can hear footsteps coming towards us,' said Josh.

'Yes, I can hear footsteps too,' said Stephen. They all froze in fear. Then it got louder and louder and they could see what it was. It was a zombie and it said, 'I want brains to eat.'

'Argh!' they all shouted, then they all ran out of the graveyard, back to Charlie's house.

The following night they decided to be brave and go back to the graveyard. When they got there they heard the sound of a train. Then they looked around and behind a tombstone they found an abandoned train carriage. It was barely visible through the tombstones and trees. It was covered with cobwebs and dead branches.

They all trembled with fear and then there was a gust of wind, the hairs on the backs of their necks stood on end as the doors of the carriage flew open, the boys hid behind the nearest tombstone as bats flew over their heads.

'This is where the zombies must have come from,' said Charlie.

'I'm not sticking around to find out, lets go,' said Stephen.

The next day they talked about what they thought they had seen and decided to go back one more time to see if it was true.

When they got to the graveyard the moon was shining brightly and there were no zombies or train carriages. 'Thank goodness for that,' they all said.

Charlie Himbury (9)
St Michael's East Wickham CE (VA) Primary School, Welling

The Terrified Ghost

One day when it was misty and foggy, a scream arose from a deserted part of Downe.

Charlie heard the scream and thought it was the wind. Then there was a knock at the door. Charlie went to open it, there was Adam!

'Hi Charlie, I thought I'd tell you about the scream. It was a ghost, the terrified ghost!'

'What is a terrified ghost?' asked Charlie.

'It's a ghost,' replied Adam.

'Why is it terrified?' said Charlie.

'Because of the Scarers, who are - a snake, two tarantulas and three vampire bats!' said Adam.

'I'm going to help the ghost,' Charlie said.

'Me too!' said Adam.

'I'll get my bits,' said Charlie, 'meet you at Downe.'

'Here we are,' Charlie whispered.

'Shall we make stuff and camouflage it?' whispered Adam.

'Yes!' said Charlie.

'There they are!' shouted Adam.

'Great, let's use our nets!' said Charlie.

'They're captured,' shouted Adam.

'Thank you,' said the ghost. 'The Scarers scared the life out of me and have terrified me ever since, so thank you very much!'

'You're welcome,' Adam and Charlie said.

'Hey, you're George!' shouted Adam.

'Yes I am. The wind blew my hood off,' said George.

'So that why you weren't at school today!' Adam said.

'Yes, you wanted to see me get rid of the Scarers,' shouted Charlie.

'I'm sorry,' said George.

'I'm going home,' said Adam.

'Me too,' yawned Charlie.

'See you both tomorrow!' shouted George.

Adam Cheshire (9)
St Michael's East Wickham CE (VA) Primary School, Welling

The Haunted House

Nobody dared to enter the spooky house, they say that a boy named Conner experienced the chill of an event.

A long time ago, Conner, aged 9, was very inquisitive and set out one night with his torch to the haunted house.

He got to the door of the house and opened it with a big creak. 'This is scary,' whispered Conner.

You could see no one had been in the haunted house for many years, there were lots of dust and cobwebs. As he began to slowly walk around and feeling airy, he felt a sense of a presence, of not being alone. Yet he still wanted to know what was in the house, he felt even more inquisitive.

'Is anybody there?' spoke Conner in a husky voice. He climbed the stairs, one by one, not knowing what or who he was going to face. He got to the top of the landing and the presence became every stronger. As he entered one of the bedrooms, he could see a bright light which made him jump, in the shape of a figure.

'Who are you?' said Conner. And there before his eyes was an elderly gentleman who had lived in the house many years ago. As he got closer, the figure began to fade …

Zoe Hickey (10)
St Michael's East Wickham
CE (VA) Primary School,
Welling

My Best Friend

On Friday the 13th, a week after my best friend Chloe died. I was walking home from school with two friends. We crossed the road where she had died when we heard a blood-curdling scream, we looked and saw blood on the road, but no one was there. We screamed as we ran into my house, breathlessly.

We watched TV but heard a creaking noise upstairs which might have been my cat. Whilst watching a horror movie, the TV went off and on and off again. We ran upstairs and played a board game. As we played, the dice rolled by itself.

Later we got into our sleeping bags, I felt like someone else was in mine. I whispered to Natalie, 'I'm scared.'

She replied, 'Why?'

I whispered that there was someone else in my sleeping bag. We started to panic but then froze when we saw my teddy floating in the air. It had turned midnight before we unfroze. We woke Katie and told her the story. It was gloomy in my bedroom and it was foggy outside.

Walking to school the next morning, we heard Chloe's voice saying 'I didn't mean to scare you, I miss you guys, can I stay with you? I promise I won't scare you anymore.'

It was odd for a while, strange things kept happening but it's only Chloe letting us know she's still around and that we're still friends.

Lauren Stokes (9)
St Michael's East Wickham CE (VA)
Primary School, Welling

The Glowing Globe

'Hello Mr Varny,' said Mr Green, as they drank their coffee.

'Where's Mr Sims?' asked Mr Varney.

(Mr Sims was actually being chased by robot ghosts, he was petrified). Mr Sims came charging into the staffroom screaming, 'Argh!' He had terror etched on his face, his skin was stark white, he felt foolish for screaming.

'What's wrong Mr Sims?' asked Mr Green.

'Ghosts are chasing me!' he exclaimed breathlessly. (They both thought his imagination had run wild!)

Mr Sims needed to lock up the school. Whilst he was walking round locking up, he heard the noise of a ghost. He ignored it, it got louder and louder and closer and closer. Mr Sims walked faster but the sound still got louder. He looked behind him and there was a real-looking ghost, not the robot one's anymore, and it had hair!

He hurriedly went round to lock up but he bumped into a desk. He looked round and on the desk was a globe, it was glowing. He picked it up and shook it. The globe started to talk to him and thundered, 'I am the one with the magical powers and I am the greatest of them all. *Ha, ha, ha!'*

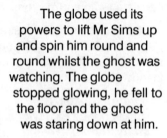

The globe used its powers to lift Mr Sims up and spin him round and round whilst the ghost was watching. The globe stopped glowing, he fell to the floor and the ghost was staring down at him.

He covered his eyes for a second, when he opened them the ghost had vanished mysteriously … Mrs Cleaver was staring down at him!

Hannah Ross (10)
St Michael's East Wickham CE (VA) Primary School, Welling

Lady In White

The lady in white is an evil, mysterious woman who wanders the Jamaica Inn. Several guests have claimed to have seen a face in their mirror, they also say they've seen a child and mother in room 5. Could the lady in white have brought a friend with her?

The owner of the Jamaica Inn called in a medium to explore. The weather was stormy and dark. The medium started on the first floor. He said, 'I don't like this room at all.'

We asked him why.

He said, 'I can feel a male in this room and he is not a very nice man, erm this might have been where he stayed.'

They couldn't find any connection to this man, so he moved onto the kitchen. He couldn't feel anything, but he could see a little boy's face in the mirror so could this little boy be the lady in white's little friend?

They moved onto the second floor, to bedroom one. Some guests have said that they get frozen in the night, but it only happens in the dead of night, so could we find the answer?

Bedroom one was where a man once stayed and I think he froze to death. So that's maybe what he's trying to tell us.

By now we were all terrified, because we were moving on to room 5 and as soon as we walked in the room, we knew we weren't wanted. The medium was even petrified, he felt she was lonely when she was alive and now she took it out on us.

After our visit to the Jamaica Inn we could now claim that it's the most haunted inn.

Grace Evans (9)
St Michael's East Wickham CE (VA) Primary School, Welling

The Castle On The Hill

Gary and Barry had a boring day and had nothing to do.

'Why don't we go and explore that castle? It is meant to be haunted!'

They started to trek up the hill. It was dark and looked gloomy. They opened the doors and entered. They were startled to see a giant spider in the hallway. The boys's eyes widened in terror!

It had been six weeks and their parents were distraught.

'The only place we haven't looked is the castle.'

The two dads set off.

The two dads opened the doors and saw two skeletons lying on the floor which were covered in blood. They went upstairs to look for the thing that had killed them. The dads heard something. They were armed with swords and daggers.

The spider was lurking in the shadows keeping its eye on them, getting its fangs ready for another feast.

As they walked past, the spider pounced. Barry's dad turned and dodged it and its fangs sank into the floor. It struggled to break free from the floorboards. Gary's dad threw a dagger that hit the spider in the back of the neck. It scampered back downstairs.

The two dads chased the spider around the house. The spider was running as fast as it could but with every drop of blood that hit the floor, it was getting weaker.

They finally caught up with the spider, jumped on its back and stabbed it in the head. It was dead and the monster of the castle was gone forever.

George Ashley (9)
St Michael's East Wickham CE (VA) Primary School, Welling

Dial-A-Ghost

That boy is so frustrating thought the middle-aged man sitting down in a chair at Dial-a-Ghost Agency. He was a very likeable man and was very kind and understanding to his little nephew, but his nephew was quite the opposite.

'You can come in now, Sir,' said the old woman opening the door.

The man got up and went through it and sitting at a wooden desk was another man.

'I have come here to order a ghost to scare my nephew out of his wits,' declared the boy's uncle.

'OK,' said the second man, 'I just need to make a few notes, such as your address and telephone number.'

The first man told the other man his number and then said, 'I'll be expecting the ghost at my house in one hour sharp.'

An hour later, there was a blood-curdling scream coming from the nephew's room and the little boy's uncle rushed upstairs to see what was happening. At first he thought the scream must mean his imagination running wild, but then he realised it must be the ghost he had ordered that morning.

He reached the top of the staircase and looked with great interest at the scene in front of him.

There were books and broken furniture all over the floor
but his nephew was not to be seen …

   Rebecca Levett (10)
   St Michael's East Wickham CE (VA) Primary School,
Welling

The Haunted House

Charlie was moving into a very old and dusty house where no one wanted to live. When he got there, his mum told him to go and have a look at his room.

He went to his bedroom and saw that there were cobwebs all over the place. The floorboards were creaky and it was stormy outside, making the room look very scary. The door suddenly slammed shut and he heard noises, so he ran downstairs and said to his mum, 'There is a ghost in my room, Mum.'

'Don't be silly,' she said, 'it is all in your imagination. Once the furniture and curtains are up, your room will look very different.'

'But I don't like the cobwebs,' said Charlie.

'Well get a duster and give your room a good dust.'

'OK Mum I'll give it a go and give it a good clean.'

The furniture men put his bed in his room but even though the room looked like his old room, he was still scared and he knew that he would have to spend the night in his scary room.

It had been a long day and Charlie's mum told him he had to go to bed. He was still scared to go to sleep but then he heard a voice. It got louder and louder, it said, 'Leave my house, if you don't you will die!'

Charlie ran to his mum's room and shouted, 'There is a ghost in my room!'

'Stop being silly,' said his mum, 'and go back to your room.'

Charlie was upset but went to his room. The ghost had started to throw his toys around the room. One of the toys hit Charlie on the head and he let out a blood-curdling scream. His head was bleeding so he ran back to his mum's room. His mum saw the cut on his head and Charlie said the ghost was throwing his toys around the room. His mum believed him this time so they very slowly went to the bedroom and the toys were floating in the air. The ghost was warning them again to leave his house.

They packed their bags straight away and left, never to return.

Andrew Taliana (9)
St Michael's East Wickham CE (VA) Primary School,
Welling

My Haunted House

In July my parents and I moved into an old house called 'The Gables'. At first I really liked living in the house but soon strange things were happening. Cupboard doors were left open, lights went on and off and things were knocked over. My mum blamed me so I set about proving that a ghost was responsible.

I started my search in the local library. I found an old book covered in cobwebs and dust and turned to the chapter marked 'The Gables'. I started to read and found what I was looking for.

A boy was sent to sweep the chimney 100 years ago and never came down. The boy was from the orphanage and had to work every day. When he disappeared, people thought he had climbed out of the chimney and run away but there were rumours that he had died and became a ghost. His name was Hector and he was 9.

I finished reading and went home to investigate.

That night I hid behind the sofa. At midnight I felt a chill and heard a glass smash on the kitchen floor. I took a deep breath and called out the boy's name. All of a sudden a head came out of the wall behind the sofa and said, 'Hello, what's your name?'

I replied, 'Charlie.' I told Hector about my problem with Mum and he agreed to stop mucking about if I played with him once in a while. We became good friends and still are.

Charlie Roberts (9)
St Michael's East Wickham
CE (VA) Primary School,
Welling

A Terrifying Thing!

Elle Dighton went to her cousin's house and they watched a scary film. Everyone was frightened except Elle. When it finished all the girls talked about the film and they all said, 'Wasn't it scary?'

'You're all babies,' Elle said.

They all went to bed and talked for a little while before they fell asleep, but Elle couldn't. She kept thinking about the film, then she heard footsteps. She knew it wasn't her aunt or uncle because they were in bed.

The room turned cold and the floorboards started to creak. Terrified couldn't explain how scared Elle was. Then she said, 'Who is it?'

A croaky voice said, 'It is I.'

Then Elle got out of bed and the ghost took her! She screamed but it was in vain.

The next morning the girls woke. 'Where's Elle?' they said.

She was nowhere to be seen …

Elle Dighton (9)
St Michael's East Wickham CE (VA) Primary School,
Welling

Nightmare In Class 5

Have you ever heard of the nightmare in Class 5 … no? Then I'll tell you.

It all started on 31st October. Sarah was making her way to her friend Sophie's house so that they and their other mate Beckie could go to their tutor group.

They walked up the hard, stone steps to Class 5. Their tutor, Mr Jones, taught them and a boy called Charlie there at 4pm.

'Sit down class,' shouted Mr Jones in his big, chilling voice.

Mr Jones was a strange man. There was something odd about him. He had dark, sunken eyes like tunnels and he had long, bony fingers. His skin was pale and cold as ice. His appearance scared the children!

Today he was even more weird. He stared at the children and started waving his cane. 'Now you, boy,' he pointed at Charlie, who was trembling and his heart was thumping behind his ribcage, 'where's your homework?'

'Errr … I f-f-forgot it Sir,' Charlie cried out, petrified, terror etched on his face.

Suddenly Mr Jones was raging, his eyes were turning red. The room went dark and the lights flickered. The children started screaming. Books and papers started zooming across the room. Sarah and Beckie's table blasted in half when a giant bolt of lightning struck it.

Sarah, Beckie and Sophie ran out, arms over their heads, ducking away from the flying books. They started to run down the stairs and suddenly they heard a blood-curdling scream.

'What was that?' cried Sophie, her lip quivering with fear.

Then they remembered something they'd forgotten. *'Charlie!'* they screamed. They hurried back up the stairs.

They stared in horror at the classroom. Standing in the doorway was what they thought was Mr Jones, holding a terrified Charlie by the throat.

'Who is th-that?' asked Sarah shakily.

'It looks like Mr Jones,' said Beckie.

'How can you tell it is?' asked Sarah.

'Touch it.'

'No way, you touch it,' said Sophie, 'it's not looking.'

Beckie crept up to the *thing* and poked it. Her hand disappeared through its stomach.

'Aaargh!' she ran away screaming, followed by her friends. Then they heard a thud and footsteps behind them. The *thing* had dropped Charlie and was running after them. Their hearts thudded in their chests. The *thing* was gaining on them. Everything was cold and misty and they couldn't see.

Suddenly, Sarah tripped and fell to the ground. The *thing* grabbed her. She began to scream, then everything went black and all was quiet. Sarah heard a voice.

'You OK Sarah? Wake up.'

'What? What? Help!' cried Sarah. She opened her eyes.

'Were you having a nightmare? You fell asleep,' asked Beckie.

'Yeah, just a dream.'

Or was it?

Hannah Fitzgerald (9)
St Michael's East Wickham CE (VA) Primary School, Welling

Was It Real?

On a dark, scary and thundery night, Charlie, Matthew and I decided to go back to school to see if the stories were true.

We set up in the library and waited for things to happen. All of a sudden, the lights started to flicker, the air turned cold and eerie. Charlie said, 'It's starting to happen.' His face was white with fright. Then there was a blood-curdling scream, everyone froze. It was coming from the basement. We all went to find out *who* and *what* it was.

On the way to the basement the lights went off. I tripped and my hand pushed a brick on the wall and a secret door opened up. I switched on my torch and found the entrance.

A green mist was coming from the room. 'I don't want to go in there!' I said.

Charlie replied, 'You stay here and be look-out.'

It was dark and gloomy, cobwebs everywhere, floorboards creaking. I pointed my torch ahead of us and there stood three shadows. I looked closer and saw the shadows more clearly, they were the ghosts of Mr Sims, Sam and Jack - the stories were true, it was the teacher and boys that never left detention!

'Ha, ha, ha, ha, ha!'

Joshua Everett (9)
St Michael's East Wickham CE (VA)
Primary School, Welling

Ghost Story

Hi, my name is Kyle Johnson but people know me by my nickname, 'Stallion'.

One day a few years ago, I gave up my job and became a street racer in Central London. I had a powerful engined gold Nissan Skyline car. No one could beat me. However one day a new racer came onto the streets and took my glory away. His name was Martin Cloud, known as 'The Phoenix'.

A few days after he had beaten me, I got my glory back because The Phoenix had a major crash and lost his life.

One year after The Phoenix died, I thought I saw his car parked in an alleyway as I drove back from my latest victory. I stopped to see if it was actually there or if I was just imagining it. I drove off but soon after, a car started to follow me. The car I had seen down the alleyway was chasing me. He started to flash his lights at me then I realised there was no one driving the car.

I stopped at some red lights and the car shot past me and disappeared. I started to drive off when I saw some white lights coming towards me. The car kept coming at me and wouldn't stop. At the last minute it swerved out of my way. I took my eyes off the road and saw the figure of The Phoenix and then I crashed.

I knew The Phoenix had tried to get his revenge.

Charlie Stott (12)
The Henry Beaufort School, Winchester

The Boy Who Wet His Pants

Stood outside the spookiest house in town, I had to listen to those kids. The gates at the entrance looked like something from the Addams' Family.

As my eyes became accustomed to the dark, inside I saw cobwebs with thick dust everywhere. There was a smell like rotting flesh. I looked around, going from room to room. The floorboards kept creaking. The furniture was covered with white cloths, making it look like ghosts.

I heard a big bang and ran to hide behind a chair. When I realised the wind had blown a door, I emerged and carried on going upstairs.

A shadow passed the door to one of the rooms so I investigated. I went through the door and heard voices, strangely like Scooby and the gang. To my surprise Scooby and Shaggy stood there eating pizza with a film crew. I walked further into the room and saw ghosts, men covered in sheets, not scary at all. The director asked me to leave.

I was walking down the stairs when I saw shadows in another room. Who was filming there? I would take a look. I saw Frankenstein, Dracula, Jeckyll and Hyde and a werewolf, sat drinking cocktails. What else would actors be doing?

They walked towards me and I thought they were going to ask me to leave just like the Scooby crew had. They didn't stop walking; they walked straight through me, real ghosts! They had spilt their cocktails on me, oh no I had wet my pants!

Michael Kenway (11)
The Henry Beaufort School,
Winchester

Hair-Raiser!

Pounding in my chest, my heart raced like a steam train. I felt the hot, fiery sensation rising in my cheeks soon spread, paralysing my whole body. Nausea washed over me and the blood charging in my ears blocked the sound of my hollow scream. All my thoughts froze in terror. I was sweating all over.

They edged closer. Backing away until my back collided with the wall, I had nowhere to run. Slowly they trudged towards me. The silence of the room was unbearable. *'Stop!'* My voice sounded so weak and it caught in my throat as I choked that single word.

This just seemed to spur them on. The large blonde leader moved quicker and all the various gingers, browns and blacks just seemed to stare up at me.

Pressing against my back was the rough brick of the barber shop wall. A breeze whistling through a gap in the door caused the bell to make a small *ding* that echoed through the empty shop and out into the night. The rain grew heavier outside.

This was when it hit me - I was alone. I was going to die alone. I was going to die alone at the mercy of old, greasy wigs.

Katherine Gazzard (12)
The Henry Beaufort
School, Winchester

Who Are You? What Are You?

I was speechless as I trembled, wanting to scream but I couldn't, I was terrified. The hairs on the back of my neck stood to attention as I began to feel tense. My feet froze as if they were in a hole of concrete.

Sat on top of a jagged stone was something evil-looking. It stared at me with these red fire-glowing eyes. The long, bony feet clenched on. It was going to charge at me like a jet plane. I didn't know what to do as I stopped dead, not able to say or do anything.

I started to shout, 'What are you? Go away!'

It didn't understand me, it was still staring at me with the red fire-glowing eyes not doing anything else.

The grass waved around as there was a gust of wind. There was a beam of light glaring down on me from the moon. It seemed like complete darkness but it was hundreds of bats flapping around. The grass just hovered around me. I didn't know what it was going to do. In my mind I was imagining me lying on the ground being covered by the overgrown, greenish grass, as the clock struck twelve in the cold, frosty night with no stars in sight.

Megan White (12)
The Henry Beaufort School, Winchester

Nightmare

As I walked down the dusty green grass, the fog rolled in over the hills. I could see dark shadows gliding over the field. They were behind me and above me. I scrambled and collapsed in a heap on the floor.

One of the black shadows was creeping towards me. I sat rooted to the ground, unable to move, even to look at its fiery red eyes. I was stuck.

It leaned over me, sensing fear and let out a high-pitched wail.

I gasped, 'What are you?'

'Your worst nightmare!' it cackled.

I looked around, they were everywhere, I could not escape, I was trapped . . .

Sam Martin (11)
The Henry Beaufort School, Winchester

Short Cut

It was pitch-black in the murky graveyard. My feet were rooted to the ground. A gloomy figure was creeping towards me. I shoved my fist towards its nose but my hand just went straight through. It was a ghost. 'It can't be,' I whispered to myself, trembling. The chalky figure bent backwards and cackled horribly.

My mother had once told me about ghosts when I was little and I was afraid to go to sleep. But that was the past. Over the years, my life became much more boring.

I screamed. The ghost tried to grab my hand but it went straight through. All around me were gravestones and bats flapping above me. I spun round and lost my balance. Suddenly, I found myself lying flat on the ground, the ghost peering down at me.

While I was lying there, I felt something move below me, a crawling sensation which reminded me of maggots. All sorts of thoughts rushed into my mind. My head felt faint, my eyelids drooped and my mouth was too dry to scream for help. I felt my heart pounding beneath my gingham shirt. I shouldn't have taken the short cut through the graveyard.

The next thing I knew, I was looking down at myself. I felt strangely calm. I was aware of a presence behind me. A beautiful, glowing figure was guarding me. The being felt strangely familiar but I couldn't work out why. From then on I knew nothing could harm me …

Rosi Keeler (11)
The Henry Beaufort School,
Winchester

Sweat

I whimpered in shock, I felt hot, really hot as if I were about to boil over like a forgotten pan on the stove, bubbling and hissing. Sweat soaked my hair and my hands felt numb. Noises overcame me, screeching and cackling like tiny witches living next to my eardrums.

Then I saw it again, the dark shadow of a tall caped person, moving swiftly through the darkness, creeping across the edge of the great flint wall. The great flint wall I was clinging to, trying desperately to disappear before the figure reached me.

'Stop please,' I whispered, not caring anymore. I wanted to wake up and it all to be a dream. It wasn't.

In the darkness I could just make out the thing's features. It was getting so close, its eyebrows raised and it looked surprised. A tear dribbled down my cheek and I collapsed, giving up.

All was silent and as I looked into the distance, tiny street lights were alive. I was mesmerised by the sudden spark of brightness. The footsteps of the creature awoke me from my hypnotised state. I felt its breath on my cheek, it was getting dreadfully close to me now and I let it. I didn't back away or run, I felt there was no point. The shadowy creature had long legs and would probably catch me up anyway. I wanted my last few moments to be relaxed, of a sort …

Poppy Trewhella (12)
The Henry Beaufort School,
Winchester

Mansion

My parents sent me to stay in Heathfield Mansion with my grandparents. We went to bed early and I was soon asleep in a luxurious four-poster bed. I woke to hear a banging noise echoing around the house. I ventured into the dark kitchen.

I was frozen in terror. All the bad dreams I had ever had in the past flashed back to me. I slipped, banging my head on the cold, hard stone of the kitchen floor. A silvery-white silhouette was gliding closer and closer. The figure was wearing a suit and tie and holding a briefcase stamped with the letters *DJB*. They were the initials of my uncle David. He died at an early age of twenty-five. I remember him only as a grumpy man, never smiling.

It suddenly became bitterly cold and the windows began to freeze over. Just as I started to scream, something forcefully blocked my mouth. It tasted bitter. A second figure with the same silvery-white glaze emerged from the darkness of the mansion kitchen. This new apparition was clad in a similar suit and tie. The two figures abruptly stopped moved and turned to look at each other.

'Who are you?' I yelled.

There was no reply, but they were advancing on me faster than ever. I tried to shuffle backwards or stand up - anything rather than coming into contact with the creatures. I did the only thing that was possible and I just ran …

Kate Symonds (11)
The Henry Beaufort School,
Winchester

Heart Of Fear

I stopped, completely stunned, my heart thumping louder than ever in my throat. My eyes fixed on the terrible sight, my feet rooted to the ground.

My sister, floating in mid-air, looked like she had fainted. Her head lolled hopelessly about. I wanted to save her, I wanted to tuck her up in bed and comfort her. My jaw dropped. What was holding her suspended - a ghost, a spirit? I didn't know.

'Jess, Jess!' I tried to scream but only a hoarse whisper came out. Suddenly someone or something was pulling me around.

It was like someone had shoved glasses on me. Our whole bedroom had been upturned but there in the middle of the room, just beyond Jess, was the thing I was dreading …

Ellie Sheahan (11)
The Henry Beaufort School, Winchester

A Trip To The Woods

I pattered through the woods, shiftily glancing from side to side. The wind whistled between the twisted, towering trees … !

Who am I kidding? All that exciting junk will never happen, not to me! As it is, I slouched through the picturesque woods with my mum and dad, gawping at every little thing they saw.

'Jodie! Look at this rock, it's an extremely strange colour!'

'No thanks Mum, I'm fine!' I yawned back. I thought about grovelling at my mum's knees, maybe then she'd take me home! I left my parents to it and went off to explore.

A few minutes later I knew I was lost - I searched for a sign back to the trail, but only found a little cottage. I sprinted to the door, hoping they had a phone and knocked twice. The entrance swung open before me and I cautiously stepped inside.

A slam from behind told me the door was shut. I knew I shouldn't waste time so I looked around the room. As soon as I moved an evil cackle issued from the corner. 'Welcome deary.'

I stood, glued to the spot. I trained my eyes on the mirror to see the witch pointing her wand at me.

Flash! My head it was like a ch-chick-chicken. As I looked, the witch shoved me into the fire. 'Mmm, chicken, wait that's me!'

The witch fell to the floor in pain. *Burning*, we wailed in unison.

'I'm the future you,' she uttered, her last words …

Eleanor Spender (12)
The Henry Beaufort School,
Winchester

Htaed Praw Graveyard

I froze; I wanted to scream but was choked by my own fear. Everything around me seemed to be watching, waiting. My imagination started to run wild, creating monsters, vampires, ghosts and other ghastly creatures that would accompany the thing. Then, from somewhere out in that cold, dark graveyard, a glimmer of light appeared from nowhere.

In a few seconds' time I would be face to face with the death warp ghost. Red eyes and a cold, dark tornado of a body, I knew only too well what it looked like. I'd seen so many pictures of it, all just as loathsome as each other. I started to feel faint. 'Take me!' I cried, 'I will be killed by my own fear if not by you.'

The ghost kept coming nearer and nearer. I screamed.

I saw the shadows of the headstones, the branches of the trees stretching out like bony fingers. I heard an owl hoot and even the air smelled of danger. I ran in blind panic without knowing where I was going. When I finally stopped I found myself back in the graveyard, where I had just been …

Laura Sharpe (11)
The Henry Beaufort School, Winchester

Horror/Fear

I was trembling, I felt like I was going to be sick. I couldn't hold it in. I was sick all down my front.

There in front of me, a dark figure with fingernails like razor-sharp knives. It was wearing a cloak and its face looked like the Devil himself.

Suddenly it was coming towards me. I backed off slowly.

'Let me be! Go away! Help, please help!' I yelled.

'No, why should I? I want to kill you!' said a rough voice. The dark figure began to laugh.

'Argh!' I woke up screaming. My bedroom door opened and there was a shadow on the wall. I felt cold and the next thing I knew, I had fainted.

When I finally woke up there was my mum and dad next to me, but there was a dark shadow behind my dad with long, razor-sharp nails …

May Sawyer (11)
The Henry Beaufort School, Winchester

Out Of Nowhere

'Huuh, huuh,' I was taking deep breaths, I couldn't move, the hairs on the back of my neck were standing on end and I could hear my teeth chattering. I grabbed the nearest gravestone for support.

I could now see an arm attached to the hand that was appearing before me. Was it a ghost? I didn't know. I wanted to run but my feet had been planted in the earth. Suddenly a head shot from the ground, causing me to nearly fall backwards.

I didn't know what to say or do. 'It can't be,' I whispered.

'Oh yes it can,' the head breathed through its smirking lips.

These words reminded me of a Punch and Judy show, a very spooky Punch and Judy show.

Without warning the ground moved. I leapt to one side and then suddenly noticed the date on the gravestone behind the head - 1376.

Now, only three words were running through my head, *The Black Prince!*

Daisy Larcombe (11)
The Henry Beaufort School, Winchester

The Werewolf

I was scared, the sweat was pouring down my face. The heat from the animal was burning my eyes. I saw a flash and I fell to the ground. My eyes felt like they had been glued to the spot.

I could hear what the beast was, then I saw it. *Oh my God!* I thought. *It's a werewolf.* I was stunned.

I tried to scramble away on the ground but nothing seemed to happen as my body was shaking so much. I closed my eyes then I heard noises! I opened my eyes, I saw it behind me. I tried to run away but it grabbed my leg, I screamed! Part of my trouser leg was torn away.

I ran, my heart was pounding, the beast was getting closer and closer. I saw lights from a house nearby. I ran but … I tripped, I wished that this was a dream but it was real life. What would happen to me now … ?

Danielle Stannard (11)
The Henry Beaufort School, Winchester

The Horror That I Saw

Sound filled the forest. Tense, I noticed everything. My feet were superglued to the leafy forest floor. Hairs on the back of my neck were raised; my heart pounded. Something moved behind me, in the mysterious shadows. I turned rapidly then stopped dead.

An almost man came out of the enclosed trees. Ready for flight, terror filled me. The man was dirty and ragged, his hair filthy and unkempt, his clothes torn and mud-covered and his face tired, worn and skeletal. At the dishevelled man's heels was a ferocious-looking dog. Its claws were inches long and its fur rough and coarse. Its teeth were sharp as icicles. Petrified, I backed away. I screamed.

'Shut up!' snarled the man. He followed my gaze. 'He won't hurt. Don't move.'

I didn't need to be told twice. I stood, stationary, hardly breathing, but managing to shoot a few glances into the immediate darkness. Except for numerous twisting, interlocking branches, there was nothing. I noticed that the man was dripping blood. His face was a mass of red cuts and his legs and arms deeply gashed. I found myself feeling sorry for him, but then I came to my senses. He looked like a murderer and a madman at that.

As my eyes tried to focus on the surreal image in front of me, it became translucent. But no. I blinked twice.

The man started to walk gradually towards me. I stood, full of fear …

Emily Cowan (11)
The Henry Beaufort
School, Winchester

Running Away From Death

Knowing that someone is following me, I keep turning around. Then I see a glimpse of a man with a sharp knife with blood on it, dripping on the brown pavement. I start running - so does the man. I see a nearby light ahead of me so I run towards it as fast as I can.

The man nearly grabs me and I trip over something sharp and rip my trousers and my leg is bleeding like mad. I get up and hobble towards the light.

For a minute, I forget about the man. I turn around he is there - hand on my shoulder, ready to stab me with his knife. I stagger up to the house's light, slapping the man's hand off me as I run into the safety of the house.

Lucy Sheridan (11)
Wetherby High School, Wetherby

The Black Candle

I expected to find some pennies under my pillow on that dreary, gloomy morning, in replacement for my bloody, battered, yellow tooth. Instead, I found this. The black candle, Now I am constrained by eeriness …

'Mum! Dad! Look what I found under my pillow! Strange or what?' I cried, trotting into the living room, the candle tight in my grasp.

Neither Mum nor Dad bothered to look up, for they were both eating slices of toast. They cared for their stomachs as much as they cared for me.

'Ignore me then!' I snapped. I stormed from the room and into the kitchen. I perched the candle on the counter and rummaged through the drawers next to the cooker. I withdrew an electric-blue lighter and set the wick of the candle alight. It hissed gently for a moment like a snake, smoke rising from the minute flames, licking at the air like a hungry tongue.

Suddenly, the candle dropped through my hands. *Butterfingers!* I thought. I kneeled down to pick it up and I yelled out like an Indian when I saw my hand, outstretched.

My hand was like sheer ice. In a sinister way, I could see through my palm to the cracked kitchen tiles! I gasped in alarm and scanned the rest of my body like a telescope searching for aliens. I was a ghost! Just like the ghosts in horror movies!

That is exactly what happens to people who mess with black candles …

Kieran Lee Newbery (12)
Ysgol Gyfun Y Strade, Llanelli

Information

We hope you have enjoyed reading this book - and that you will continue to enjoy it in the coming years.

If you like reading and writing drop us a line, or give us a call, and we'll send you a free information pack.

Write to:
Young Writers Information, Remus House, Coltsfoot Drive, Woodston, Peterborough PE2 9JX Tel: 01733 890066 or check out our website at www.youngwriters.co.uk.